ILLUSTRATED COURSE GUIDES

AF901524

Professionalism

SECOND EDITION

ILLUSTRATED COURSE GUIDES

Professionalism

SECOND EDITION

Jeff Butterfield

Cengage

Australia • Brazil • Canada • Mexico • Singapore • United Kingdom • United States

Cengage

Professionalism, 2nd Edition: Illustrated Course Guides
Jeff Butterfield

Product Director: Kathleen McMahon

Associate Product Manager: Reed Curry

Associate Content Developer: Maria Garguilo

Marketing Director: Michele McTighe

Marketing Manager: Jeff Tousignant

Marketing Coordinator: Cassie Cloutier

Contributing Author: Lisa Ruffolo

Developmental Editor: Lisa Ruffolo

Content Project Manager: Jen Feltri-George

IP Analyst: Amber Hill

Senior IP Project Manager: Kathy Kucharek

Proofreader: Brandy Lilly

Indexer: Elizabeth Cunningham

Print Buyer: Fola Orekoya

Composition: Lumina Datamatics Inc.

Art Director: Diana Graham

Cover Template Designer: Lisa Kuhn, Curio Press, LLC www.curiopress.com

Text Designer: GEX Publishing Services

For product information and technology assistance, contact us at
Cengage Customer & Sales Support, 1-800-354-9706
or support.cengage.com.

For permission to use material from this text or product, submit all requests online at **www.copyright.com.**

Library of Congress Control Number: 2016938486

ISBN-13: 978-1-337-11926-9
ISBN-10: 1-337-11926-1

Cengage
200 Pier 4 Boulevard
Boston, MA 02210
USA

Figure A-1 © Monkey Business Images, 2009. Used under license from Shutterstock.com; Figure C-18 © Yuri Arcurs, 2009. Used under license from Shutterstock.com; all other photos © Jupiterimages Corporation.

Printed in the United States of America
Print Number: 07 Print Year: 2022

About the Series

Students work hard to earn certificates and degrees to prepare for a particular career—but do they have the soft skills necessary to succeed in today's digital workplace? Can they communicate effectively? Present themselves professionally? Work in a team? Industry leaders agree there is a growing need for these essential soft skills; in fact, they are critical to a student's success in the workplace. Without them, they will struggle and even fail. However, students entering the workforce who can demonstrate strong soft skills have a huge competitive advantage.

The *Illustrated Course Guides—Soft Skills for a Digital Workplace* series is designed to help you teach these important skills, better preparing your students to enter a competitive marketplace. Here are some of the key elements you will find in each book in the series:

- **Focused content allows for flexibility:** Each book in the series is short, focused, and covers only the most essential skills related to the topic. You can use the modular content in standalone courses or workshops or you can integrate it into existing courses.
- **Visual design keeps students engaged:** Our unique pedagogical design presents each skill on two facing pages, with key concepts and instructions on the left and illustrations on the right. This keeps students of all levels on track.
- **Varied activities put skills to the test:** Each book includes hands-on activities, team exercises, critical thinking questions, and scenario-based activities to allow students to put their skills to work and demonstrate their retention of the material.

Read the Preface for more details on the key pedagogical elements and features of this book. We hope the books in this series help your students gain the critical soft skills they need to succeed in whatever career they choose.

Advisory Board

We thank our Advisory Board who gave us their opinions and guided our decisions as we developed the first titles in this series. They are as follows:

Debi Griggs, Instructor of Business and Business Technology, Bellevue College
Jean Insinga, Professor of Information Systems, Middlesex Community College
Gary Marrer, CIS Faculty, Glendale Community College
Linda Meccouri, Professor, Springfield Technical Community College
Lynn Wermers, Chair, Computer and Information Sciences, North Shore Community College
Nancy Wilson Head, Executive Director Teaching & Learning Technologies, Purdue University

Preface

Welcome to *Professionalism, Second Edition: Illustrated Course Guides*. If this is your first experience with the Illustrated Course Guides, you'll see that this book has a unique design: each skill is presented on two facing pages, with Essential Elements on the left and illustrations and examples pictured on the right. The layout makes it easy to learn a skill without having to read a lot of text and flip pages to see an illustration. The design also makes this a great reference after the course is over! See the illustration on the right to learn more about the pedagogical and design elements of a typical lesson.

Focused on the Essentials

Each two-page lesson presents only the most important information about the featured lesson skill. The left page of the lesson presents 5 or 6 key Essential Elements, which are the most important guidelines that a student needs to know about the skill. Absorbing and retaining a limited number of key ideas makes it more likely that students will retain and apply the skill in a real-life situation.

Hands-On Activities

Every lesson contains a You Try It exercise, where students demonstrate their understanding of the lesson skill by completing a task that relates to it. The steps in the You Try It exercises are often general, requiring that students use critical thinking to complete the task.

Real World Advice and Examples

To help put lesson skills in context, many lessons contain yellow shaded boxes that present real-world stories pulled from today's workplace. Some lessons also contain Do's and Don'ts tables, featuring key guidelines on what to do and not do in certain workplace situations relating to the lesson skill. The Technology@Work lesson at the end of every unit covers Web 2.0 tools and other technologies relating to the unit.

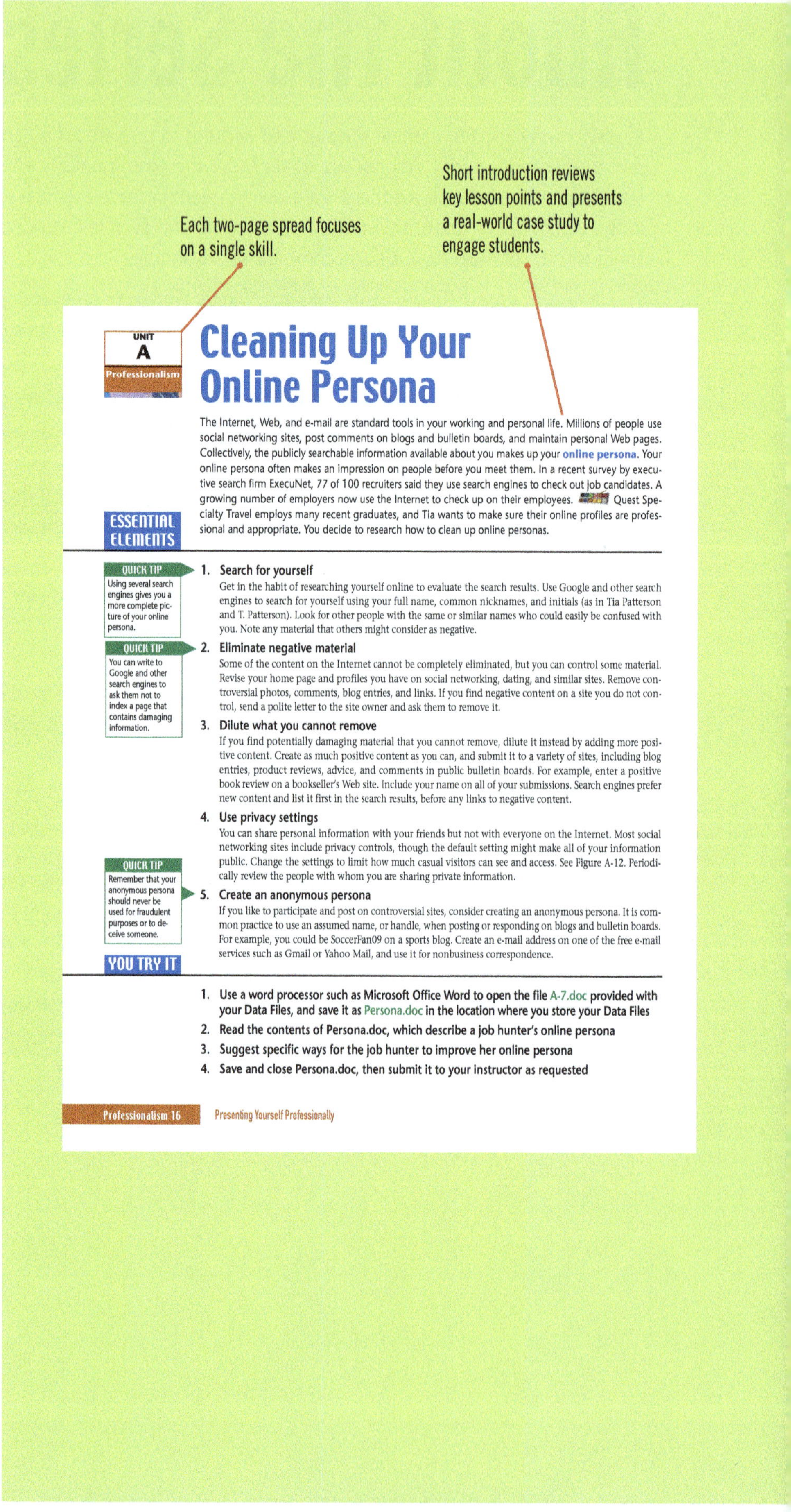

Cleaning Up Your Online Persona

The Internet, Web, and e-mail are standard tools in your working and personal life. Millions of people use social networking sites, post comments on blogs and bulletin boards, and maintain personal Web pages. Collectively, the publicly searchable information available about you makes up your **online persona**. Your online persona often makes an impression on people before you meet them. In a recent survey by executive search firm ExecuNet, 77 of 100 recruiters said they use search engines to check out job candidates. A growing number of employers now use the Internet to check up on their employees. Quest Specialty Travel employs many recent graduates, and Tia wants to make sure their online profiles are professional and appropriate. You decide to research how to clean up online personas.

QUICK TIP: Using several search engines gives you a more complete picture of your online persona.

QUICK TIP: You can write to Google and other search engines to ask them not to index a page that contains damaging information.

QUICK TIP: Remember that your anonymous persona should never be used for fraudulent purposes or to deceive someone.

1. **Search for yourself**
   Get in the habit of researching yourself online to evaluate the search results. Use Google and other search engines to search for yourself using your full name, common nicknames, and initials (as in Tia Patterson and T. Patterson). Look for other people with the same or similar names who could easily be confused with you. Note any material that others might consider as negative.
2. **Eliminate negative material**
   Some of the content on the Internet cannot be completely eliminated, but you can control some material. Revise your home page and profiles you have on social networking, dating, and similar sites. Remove controversial photos, comments, blog entries, and links. If you find negative content on a site you do not control, send a polite letter to the site owner and ask them to remove it.
3. **Dilute what you cannot remove**
   If you find potentially damaging material that you cannot remove, dilute it instead by adding more positive content. Create as much positive content as you can, and submit it to a variety of sites, including blog entries, product reviews, advice, and comments in public bulletin boards. For example, enter a positive book review on a bookseller's Web site. Include your name on all of your submissions. Search engines prefer new content and list it first in the search results, before any links to negative content.
4. **Use privacy settings**
   You can share personal information with your friends but not with everyone on the Internet. Most social networking sites include privacy controls, though the default setting might make all of your information public. Change the settings to limit how much casual visitors can see and access. See Figure A-12. Periodically review the people with whom you are sharing private information.
5. **Create an anonymous persona**
   If you like to participate and post on controversial sites, consider creating an anonymous persona. It is common practice to use an assumed name, or handle, when posting or responding on blogs and bulletin boards. For example, you could be SoccerFan09 on a sports blog. Create an e-mail address on one of the free e-mail services such as Gmail or Yahoo Mail, and use it for nonbusiness correspondence.

YOU TRY IT

1. **Use a word processor such as Microsoft Office Word to open the file A-7.doc provided with your Data Files, and save it as Persona.doc in the location where you store your Data Files**
2. **Read the contents of Persona.doc, which describe a job hunter's online persona**
3. **Suggest specific ways for the job hunter to improve her online persona**
4. **Save and close Persona.doc, then submit it to your instructor as requested**

Professionalism 16 Presenting Yourself Professionally

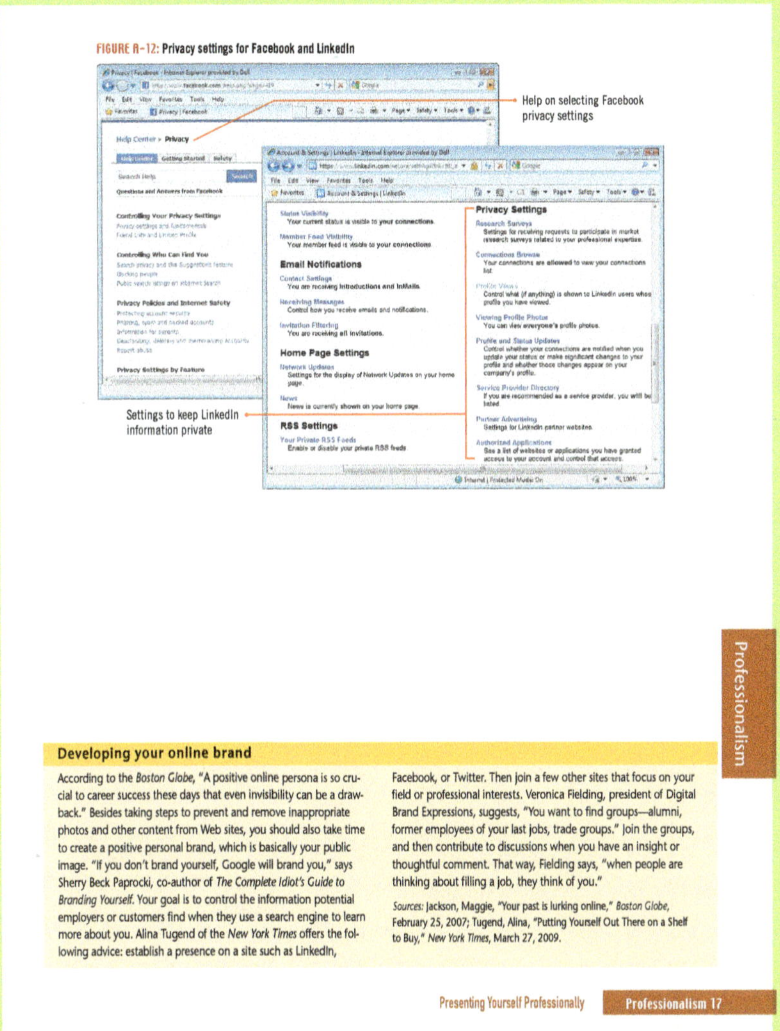

FIGURE A-12: Privacy settings for Facebook and LinkedIn

Developing your online brand

According to the *Boston Globe*, "A positive online persona is so crucial to career success these days that even invisibility can be a drawback." Besides taking steps to prevent and remove inappropriate photos and other content from Web sites, you should also take time to create a positive personal brand, which is basically your public image. "If you don't brand yourself, Google will brand you," says Sherry Beck Paprocki, co-author of *The Complete Idiot's Guide to Branding Yourself*. Your goal is to control the information potential employers or customers find when they use a search engine to learn more about you. Alina Tugend of the *New York Times* offers the following advice: establish a presence on a site such as LinkedIn, Facebook, or Twitter. Then join a few other sites that focus on your field or professional interests. Veronica Fielding, president of Digital Brand Expressions, suggests, "You want to find groups—alumni, former employees of your last jobs, trade groups." Join the groups, and then contribute to discussions when you have an insight or thoughtful comment. That way, Fielding says, "when people are thinking about filling a job, they think of you."

Sources: Jackson, Maggie, "Your past is lurking online," *Boston Globe*, February 25, 2007; Tugend, Alina, "Putting Yourself Out There on a Shelf to Buy," *New York Times*, March 27, 2009.

Presenting Yourself Professionally   Professionalism 17

Lessons and Exercises

The lessons use Quest Specialty Travel, a fictional adventure travel company, as the case study. The assignments on the light purple pages at the end of each unit increase in difficulty. Data files and case studies provide a variety of interesting and relevant business applications. Assignments include:

- **Soft Skills Reviews** provide multiple choice questions that test students' understanding of the unit material.
- **Critical Thinking Questions** pose topics for discussion that require analysis and evaluation. Many also challenge students to consider and react to realistic critical thinking and application of the unit skills.
- **Independent Challenges** are case projects requiring critical thinking and application of the unit skills.
- **Real Life Independent Challenges** are practical exercises where students can apply the skills they learned in an activity that will help their own lives. For instance, they might analyze decisions they need to make, such as which job offer to accept, whether to buy a house or rent an apartment, and whether to continue their formal education.
- **Team Challenges** are practical projects that require working together in a team to solve a problem.
- **Be the Critic Exercises** are activities that require students to evaluate a flawed example and provide ideas for improving it.

Instructor Resources

The Instructor Resources provide instructors with a wide range of tools that enhance teaching and learning. These resources and more can be accessed from the instructor companion site. Log in at www.cengage.com/SSO.

- **Instructor's Manual**—Written by the author and available as an electronic file, the Instructor's Manual is a valuable teaching tool for your course. It includes detailed lecture topics with teaching tips for each unit.
- **Sample Syllabus**—Prepare and customize your course easily using this sample course outline.
- **PowerPoint Presentations**—Each unit has a corresponding PowerPoint presentation that you can use in lecture, distribute to your students, or customize to suit your course.
- **Solutions to Exercises**—Solutions to Exercises contains every file students are asked to create or modify in the lessons and end-of-unit material. This section also includes a solutions to the Soft Skills Reviews and Independent Challenges.
- **Data Files for Students**—To complete most of the units in this book, your students will need Data Files. You can post the Data Files on a file server for students to copy. The Data Files can be downloaded from www.cengage.com.
- **Test Banks**—Cengage Learning Testing powered by Cognero is a flexible, online system that allows instructors to author, edit, and manage test bank content from multiple Cengage Learning solutions and to create multiple versions. It works on any operating system or browser with no special installs or downloads needed, so tests can be created from anywhere with Internet access.

Brief Contents

Contents

UNIT
A
Professionalism

Presenting Yourself Professionally

Files You Will Need:

A-1.doc
A-2.doc
A-3.doc
A-4.doc
A-5.doc
A-6.doc
A-7.doc
A-8.doc
A-9.doc

Without conscious effort, other people are regularly observing and evaluating you. People use these impressions to anticipate and plan their interactions with you and others in their personal and professional life. For example, they make judgments about your manner of dress, speaking style, choice of words, behavior, and job performance. Studies suggest that most people form opinions about a new acquaintance within the first minute or two of interaction. Ideally, you want to create positive impressions with those you encounter. Taking the time to present yourself favorably helps you to get noticed and positively influence others. The effort also helps you feel better about yourself and improves your attitude and confidence. In this unit, you will learn how to present yourself professionally. Quest Specialty Travel (QST) is expanding its New York branch and recently named Tia Patterson as the director. You work as Tia's assistant and primarily help her with personnel tasks, including hiring and training. Tia wants to develop a training session on professional image, and asks you to concentrate on learning how to present yourself professionally so you can train your colleagues to do the same.

OBJECTIVES

Manage your image
Dress appropriately
Meet business casual standards
Maintain a professional wardrobe
Practice good grooming and hygiene
Interact with others
Improve your speech
Clean up your online persona

UNIT A

Professionalism

Managing Your Image

Your **image** is how you combine clothing, grooming, behavior, and speech to represent yourself to others. Cultivating an image balances personal expression with social customs. You can express yourself through how you dress, for example, though your choices are limited to what is socially acceptable. In your private life, you usually have the freedom to present the type of image you want. However, when you accept employment with an organization, your employer expects you to conform to established norms and dress codes. How you present yourself and manage your image influences your professional relationships and the progress you make in your career. Tia Patterson suggests you review the basics of managing your professional image.

DETAILS

How you present yourself influences your professional relationships for the following reasons:

- **Your image is the sum of your observable characteristics**
  The people you work with form impressions about you based on characteristics they can observe, such as your appearance, speaking, writing, and performance. They evaluate you not only in formal and professional settings, but informal settings as well. See Figure A-1. Be conscious of this impression so you can define the type of image that you want to project.
- **Your presentation signals your role in the organization**
  Your personal appearance and image help colleagues and decision makers understand your role in the organization. People with a significant amount of responsibility are expected to dress and act more formally. A chief executive officer (CEO) of a company typically dresses differently from someone who works in the warehouse. The CEO's clothing, grooming, and mannerisms should set him or her apart from the rest of the organization to reflect his or her responsibilities, status, and role as a leader.
- **Your image affects your career path**
  Your image affects decisions that are made about whether you should be promoted or given additional job responsibility. A classic piece of career advice is to dress for the next position you are seeking. If you look the part, the promotion decision is easier to make. See Figure A-2. People who dress too casually are often not considered for advancement opportunities.
- **Your image reflects that of your company**
  When you meet with clients, industry partners, suppliers, and other external **stakeholders**, they form impressions about your company based on you and how you present yourself. Organizations frequently have different dress codes for sales people, media relations, and others that regularly interact with the public.
- **Your appearance influences how you feel about yourself**
  The way you dress and carry yourself significantly affects your confidence and self-esteem. When you are dressed appropriately for the occasion, you feel more comfortable and can focus on the tasks at hand. Someone who is underdressed, or out of step with the company norms, is more likely to be self-conscious and uncomfortable in important encounters, meetings, and presentations.

QUICK TIP
A stakeholder is someone who plays a central role in a project, problem, or decision and has an interest in its outcome.

FIGURE A-1: How you present yourself influences your professional relationships

© Monkey Business Images/ShutterStock.com

FIGURE A-2: Image affects your career path

© Jupiterimages Corporation

Professional image = career success

Online sites for job seekers emphasize that projecting a professional image helps you land a job and build a career. Dressing for success starts with the first interview. CareerBuilder.com gives the following advice: "Save 'innovative' or revealing garb for the club (or your couch) and strive for crisp, clean, and professional. Remember, you want the interviewer to be listening to what you're saying, not critiquing what you're wearing." A CareerBuilder.com survey also asked employers about image and appearance. 41 percent said employees who dressed professionally tended to be promoted more often than others in their organization.

Furthermore, how you look on the outside directly affects your attitude. Consider the success story of Jasmine Lawrence from Williamstown, New Jersey. When she was a young teen, chemical hair-care products caused much of her hair to fall out. After researching natural alternatives, she started Eden Body Works, a company specializing in all-natural hair and skin care products. As a junior in high school, Jasmine negotiated a deal with Wal-Mart to sell her products nationwide, and now earns over $1 million in revenue. According to Jasmine, her transformation began with her wardrobe. "At first, it was a challenge to fit in—in the jungle of corporate America . . . I needed a professional attitude that would gain me respect among adults. I also needed professional attire . . . I started my businesswoman transformation with my wardrobe. I knew that I had to look the part if I planned to run a multimillion-dollar empire one day. So, I went out and bought suits for all occasions. I also went into my closet and pulled out the shoes that I usually wore only on special occasions. I stood up straight, looked in the mirror, and saw the businesswoman I was destined to be." As Mark Twain said, "Clothes make the man"—or woman.

Sources: Haefner, Rosemary, "Dressing for Success at Work," *www.careerbuilder.com*, accessed September 29, 2009; Staff, "A High School Senior Sells into Wal-Mart," *www.businessweek.com*, published October 3, 2008.

UNIT

A

Professionalism

Dressing Appropriately

In previous generations, dress codes for professional workers were fairly standard. What was known as **international standard business** attire included suits, jackets, dresses, long-sleeved shirts, ties, and leather shoes. Although many companies still use this as their dress code, business apparel now trends more casual. Today, there is no single standard dress code for the workplace. Expectations differ according to the position you hold, the company's culture, industry norms, and even geographic region. Table A-1 summarizes the do's and don'ts for dressing appropriately. Tia asks you to outline guidelines for dressing appropriately in a professional setting.

ESSENTIAL ELEMENTS

1. **Clarify expectations before you start**
   Before starting a job, ask your new manager or the human resources staff about the company's dress codes and practical expectations for someone in your position. Don't rely on your own casual observations made during the interview. You might have visited the company on "blue jean Friday" and formed the wrong impression.

QUICK TIP
Your appearance should be appropriate for the group that you work with.

2. **Consider your department**
   Although a company might publish a dress code or standards, expectations can still vary among departments and divisions. For example, creative workers such as designers, artists, and photographers are often allowed to dress casually. Accountants, on the other hand, tend to dress conservatively, even when working at a company with casual norms. See Figure A-3.

3. **Respect industry norms**
   Some industries have traditions and norms for how professionals in the field should dress. For example, consider how differently you expect people from the banking, healthcare, and music recording industries to dress. Even if your company has a casual dress code, your customers may have more formal expectations because of your industry.

QUICK TIP
Adjust to where you are living and working, and be prepared to change if you have to travel or move.

4. **Follow standards for your location**
   Norms for professional dress often vary by location. What is acceptable in Los Angeles or San Francisco might be too casual in New York or Boston. Even within a company, the accepted culture at the main headquarters is often different from that at a distant branch office.

5. **Err on the formal side**
   A good rule to follow is to start a new job by dressing formally and then adjust as you become integrated into the organization. Wearing a business suit on your first day at the office, for example, makes a positive impression when you are introduced to new colleagues and managers. You can remove a jacket or tie if you need to look more casual.

6. **Remember that your employer sets the standards**
   Students generally enjoy freedom in terms of their dress and grooming while in school. Some mistakenly assume that they should have the same latitude after they graduate and start their careers. In the United States (and many other countries), employers have the legal right to expect you to adhere to a dress code and to have separate dress and grooming standards for men and women.

YOU TRY IT

1. Use a word processor such as Microsoft Office Word to open the file A-1.doc provided with your Data Files, and save it as Appropriate.doc in the location where you store your Data Files
2. Read the contents of Appropriate.doc, which describe a business situation
3. Use the guidelines in this lesson to list the appropriate elements of the employee's dress and actions
4. Save and close Appropriate.doc, then submit it to your instructor as requested

FIGURE A-3: Dress codes can differ by department

© Jupiterimages Corporation

Design department

© Jupiterimages Corporation

Accounting department

TABLE A-1: Dressing appropriately do's and don'ts

guideline	do	don't
Clarify expectations	• Learn what is appropriate for you and dress accordingly • Ask about the dress code in your organization	**Don't** rely on the observations you made when interviewing
Consider your department, industry, and location	• Dress to match other members of your department or division • Observe the traditions and norms for your field or profession • Follow the standards for your geographic location	• **Don't** assume the style of dress in one department or job type is appropriate for another • **Don't** dress casually if your customers expect more formal attire, even if your company has a casual dress code
Start formally	Dress formally at first, then adjust to match the norms in the organization	**Don't** start informally and then dress up to meet expectations—first impressions are lasting ones
Follow your employer's standards	Remember that your employer sets the standards for work attire	**Don't** assume you can dress for work as you did for school

UNIT
A
Professionalism

Meeting Business Casual Standards

Many businesses adopt a relaxed dress code commonly called **business casual**. This style usually means clothes less formal than a traditional suit and tie, yet dressier than jeans and a t-shirt. Because many types and styles of clothing fall between those two extremes, organizations often interpret the business casual standard differently. In addition, the word "casual" can be misleading, so people assume that comfortable and convenient dress of any type is appropriate. Instead, business casual clothing should be clean, dressy, and suitable to your work environment. Table A-2 lists the do's and don'ts for meeting business casual standards. Quest Specialty Travel uses business casual as its dress code. Tia asks you to describe the standards of business casual dressing.

ESSENTIAL ELEMENTS

QUICK TIP
Owning two suits in different colors gives your wardrobe some flexibility.

1. **Have at least two business suits**
   Even if you plan on working for a company where casual dress is the norm, you should still own two conservative business suits. The material should be either a solid color or subtle pinstripe made of wool or wool blend. Navy and gray are classic colors for business apparel. Wear a white long-sleeve buttoned shirt or a coordinated blouse under the jacket. Men should wear a conservative tie. You should also wear professional shoes and socks or stockings.

2. **Dress more formally for job interviews and important events**
   When dressing for a job interview, career fair, or other recruiting function, wear a business suit. Do so even if the interviewing manager will be dressed in business casual. A suit helps you look the part of a career-minded professional and shows respect to the person you are meeting.

QUICK TIP
The term "casual" in "business casual" does not mean that your appearance should be careless. Your goal is to look professional and polished.

3. **Wear appropriate attire for business casual**
   The business casual style is more flexible than business formal, but more conservative than at-home wear. Figure A-4 shows common elements of business casual. Some organizations may insist on long-sleeve shirts (even in summer months) or encourage shirts embroidered with a company logo. Learn which elements your employer favors and dress accordingly.

QUICK TIP
You should also dress up for key meetings, visits with clients, and other important events even if you otherwise wear business casual.

4. **Dress more formally than what is expected**
   Some people push the limits of what is acceptable casual wear on the job, without overtly violating company standards. You will benefit from dressing slightly better than what is normal for your department. This might be as simple as wearing a tie when others have open collars, or wearing long-sleeve dress shirts when others wear polo shirts.

5. **Avoid inappropriate clothing**
   When given the opportunity to wear business casual, remember that certain pieces of clothing are not appropriate for business wear. Avoid shorts, jeans (unless specifically allowed), athletic shoes and sneakers, sandals, t-shirts, athletic apparel, short dresses and skirts, tops that are low or revealing, and any clothing that is worn or wrinkled. Emphasize the "business" part of business casual.

YOU TRY IT

1. **Use a word processor such as Microsoft Office Word to open the file A-2.doc provided with your Data Files, and save it as Business Casual.doc in the location where you store your Data Files**
2. **Read the contents of Business Casual.doc, which describe a business meeting**
3. **Complete the lists included in the document to identify the clothing that meets or does not meet business casual standards**
4. **Save and close Business Casual.doc, then submit it to your instructor as requested**

FIGURE A-4: Examples of business casual

TABLE A-2: Dressing appropriately do's and don'ts

guideline	do	don't
Dress formally when necessary	• Have at least two business suits you can wear when necessary • Wear a business suit for job interviews, recruiting events, and other special occasions	• **Don't** overlook accessories such as shoes and socks when dressing formally • **Don't** dress down for a job interview, even if the interviewer will be dressed casually
Follow business casual standards	• Choose clothes that are conservative, modest, and well coordinated • Pay attention to your employer's standards, and dress accordingly	• **Don't** assume "casual" means informal • **Don't** overlook your employer's guidelines
Dress more formally than expectations	Dress slightly better than what is normal for your department	**Don't** push the limits of acceptable casual attire by wearing shorts, athletic shoes, sandals, or t-shirts

Business casual: Common but not well understood

According to a recent Gallup poll on work and education, 43% of full- or part-time employees wear business casual clothing to work most days, while 28% wear casual street clothes, 19% wear a uniform, and only 9% wear formal business clothing. Yet "business casual" is difficult to define, and varies from one organization to another. For players engaged in team business, the National Basketball Association defines business casual as "A long or short-sleeved dress shirt (collared or turtleneck), and/or a sweater, dress slacks, khaki pants, or dress jeans, and appropriate shoes and socks, including dress shoes, dress boots, or other presentable shoes, but not including sneakers, sandals, flip-flops, or work boots." Other organizations are more general. For example, Ford Motor Company has a business casual dress code that boils down to using good judgment, says Marcey Evans, a Ford spokeswoman. The current trend seems to favor conservative attire. "I see a return to more traditional business wear," said Gary Brody, president of the Marcraft Apparel Group. "People dress up more in times of financial uncertainty and intense competition. It helps their sense of stability." Whether business casual or otherwise, professional attire is neat, clean, and in good repair. Remember that you generally can't go wrong if you dress for the job you want, so if your goal is to be a department manager, dress like the department managers do.

Sources: Finney, Paul Burnham, "Redefining Business Casual," *The New York Times*, October 23, 2007;
Gallup News Service, "'Business Casual' Most Common Work Attire," *www.gallup.com*, October 4, 2007.

UNIT A
Professionalism

Maintaining a Professional Wardrobe

The clothing that you buy for business use is an investment in your professional career. Try to buy well-constructed clothing in classic styles; it'll prove to be economical in the long run. Inexpensive items often use lower thread counts and fabric weights to keep the material costs low. However, such clothing does not stand up well to repeated wash and wear. Pay attention to your wardrobe and maintain your clothes properly. This extends the life of your clothes and makes each item look neater and more finished. Table A-3 summarizes the do's and don'ts of maintaining a professional wardrobe. Now that you and Tia have a better idea of what business casual means, she asks you to research the basics of maintaining a professional wardrobe.

ESSENTIAL ELEMENTS

QUICK TIP
Liquid detergents tend to dissolve more effectively in water than powdered soaps.

1. **Launder your own clothing**
   Having your clothing professionally cleaned can be very expensive. When you launder your own clothes, do so according to the care label on the garment. See Figure A-5. If clothes are machine-washable, separate colors, whites, and delicate items into different loads. Keep clothing with red tones separate from other garments so the red dye does not bleed into other items. Use a suitable laundry detergent, and follow the instructions carefully.

2. **Protect your colors**
   Each time you launder a piece of clothing, you increase the wear on the fabric and its color. When washing whites, add bleach to help remove stains and brighten the clothes. Turning colored articles inside out reduces color wear. Drying your clothing on a line takes longer than a dryer, but also reduces the deterioration of the fabric.

3. **Dry-clean or hand wash when appropriate**
   Some items of clothing are not designed for the washing machine. Business suits, silk shirts and ties, woolens, and similar items should be professionally dry-cleaned. You can hand wash some synthetics and delicate clothing using a mild detergent designed for this purpose. Hang hand-washed garments to dry or lay them across a horizontal drying rack or net.

QUICK TIP
Experiment with different amounts of starch to find the amount of body that you like.

4. **Give your clothing a pressed look**
   Properly ironing and hanging your clothing creates a neat, pressed appearance. See Figure A-6. Ironing is best done when clothes are almost, but not quite dry. Remove clothes from the dryer promptly to avoid wrinkling. Add starch to the rinse cycle or spray liquid sizing when you iron to add a crisp finish to clothes and help them resist wrinkling throughout the day.

QUICK TIP
Keep a travel shoe kit in your desk to fix scuffs while at work.

5. **Maintain your shoes**
   Wear leather dress shoes in professional environments. Insert shoe trees when you remove your shoes to help them keep their shape. Wearing a different pair of shoes on alternate days also preserves the leather. Use a shoe shine kit regularly to clean and condition your shoes. Shoes that are dull, scuffed, or scratched can ruin an otherwise professional appearance.

YOU TRY IT

1. **Use a word processor such as Microsoft Office Word to open the file A-3.doc provided with your Data Files, and save it as Wardrobe.doc in the location where you store your Data Files**
2. **Read the contents of Wardrobe.doc, which describe an employee's weekly routine**
3. **Complete the table in the document to evaluate how well the employee maintains her wardrobe**
4. **Save and close Wardrobe.doc, then submit it to your instructor as requested**

FIGURE A-5: Care tag on a garment

FIGURE A-6: Press and hang your clothes

TABLE A-3: Maintaining a professional wardrobe do's and don'ts

guideline	do	don't
Launder your clothes	• Wash and dry clothes according to instructions on the care label • Separate colors, whites, and delicate items into different loads • Use laundry detergent according to manufacturer's instructions, especially for measuring the proper amount • Protect colored clothes by turning them inside-out • Use a tape roll or brush to remove pet hair or lint	• **Don't** forget to wash garments after wearing them once or twice • **Don't** wash cotton clothing in hot water • **Don't** machine-wash delicate garments or those marked as dry-clean only
Iron and hang your clothes	• Iron clothes when they are slightly damp and almost dry • Remove clothes from the dryer promptly • Use starch or liquid sizing to add a crisp finish to clothes	• **Don't** wear wrinkled or rumpled garments • **Don't** lay ironed clothes on a horizontal surface; hang them to prevent wrinkling
Maintain your shoes	• Wear leather dress shoes in professional environments • When you remove leather shoes, insert shoe trees so the shoes keep their shape • Polish and condition your shoes regularly	**Don't** wear shoes that are dull, scuffed, or scratched

Maintaining a professional wardrobe while traveling

Many jobs involve travel to meet clients and potential customers, attend conferences and trade shows, or work with colleagues at another company location. When you're traveling on business, you want to dress for comfort while still maintaining a professional appearance. To avoid extra expenses for checked luggage, many business travelers prefer to use only carry-on bags, which means you need to pack lightly. If you need a variety of clothing types when you arrive, plan your travel wardrobe carefully. For example, on a business trip involving a series of meetings with the same group of people over the course of four days, you can pack two suits. Include four sets of varied shirts and accessories so it doesn't seem like you are wearing the same outfit four days in a row. If you are meeting with different people over those four days, you could repeat an outfit one or two days. Make sure the outfits you choose coordinate with your dress shoes so you don't have to pack more than one extra pair. Choose shoes that are professional but comfortable because you usually walk more when traveling. To look crisp and neat during your meetings, be sure to select wrinkle-resistant fabrics, fold clothes to prevent creases, unpack as soon as possible, press out any wrinkles, and then hang your clothes for the next day.

Practicing Good Grooming and Hygiene

Personal hygiene is the practice of maintaining cleanliness and health. You need to develop some hygiene habits such as hand washing to protect against illness and disease. Other practices such as grooming your hair are dictated by cultural standards. Overall, you should use proper personal hygiene to enhance social and professional interactions. Develop daily habits that cover personal hygiene and grooming basics to make sure you are healthy and create an appealing impression. Table A-4 lists the do's and don'ts for practicing good grooming and hygiene. In addition to maintaining a professional wardrobe, Tia says employees also need to maintain high standards for hygiene and grooming. She suggests you outline these standards for the employees.

ESSENTIAL ELEMENTS

QUICK TIP
A shower after physical activity is also a good idea.

1. **Bathe every day**

   A shower or bath keeps you refreshed and clean, and should be part of your daily routine. Use deodorant or antiperspirant after bathing. If you use scented products such as soap or shampoo, keep in mind that many people are sensitive to fragrances, especially when combined. Choose lightly scented or unscented products and coordinate the fragrances so they are not distracting.

QUICK TIP
Facial hair is acceptable in most industries as long as it is short and neatly trimmed.

2. **Groom facial hair**

   Men can choose whether to shave regularly or maintain a beard or moustache. In either case, you should groom your facial hair at least once a day. If you shave, make sure you do so in the same direction the hair grows. Use a moisturizing shaving cream instead of soap and water, which can dry your skin. Condition your face by using a moisturizing aftershave. If you have a beard or moustache, trim it neatly so it keeps its shape. A barber can trim your facial hair professionally, though you can do it yourself with a cordless beard trimmer (not scissors). See Figure A-7.

3. **Care for your hair**

   To groom your hair, shampoo often enough to keep your hair looking and smelling clean. Most people shampoo daily, though if your hair is dry or very curly, you can shampoo less often. Use a shampoo and conditioner designed to be healthy for your scalp and hair type. Brush or comb your hair at the beginning of the day and when it becomes tangled or windblown. As with your clothes, choose conservative hair styles that match your job and position. See Figure A-8.

QUICK TIP
Use mints to freshen your breath before talking to someone.

4. **Keep your breath fresh**

   Brush your teeth regularly for dental health and for fresh breath. Dental professionals advise you to floss daily and to brush your tongue, which can harbor bacteria that causes bad breath. After drinking or eating anything with an odor such as coffee, onions, or spiced food, brush your teeth and use a mouthwash if possible.

5. **Maintain foot health**

   While showering or bathing, wash your feet and then dry them thoroughly to eliminate odors and prevent athlete's foot. In addition, you can dust your shoes with foot powder and allow them to air out after you wear them. Wear comfortable, well-fitting socks or stockings, and change them at least once a day.

YOU TRY IT

1. Use a word processor such as Microsoft Office Word to open the file A-4.doc provided with your Data Files, and save it as Hygiene.doc in the location where you store your Data Files
2. Read the contents of Hygiene.doc, which describe an employee's daily routine
3. Complete the table in the document to evaluate the employee's grooming habits
4. Save and close Hygiene.doc, then submit it to your instructor as requested

FIGURE A-7: Well-groomed professionals

© Jupiterimages Corporation

© Jupiterimages Corporation

FIGURE A-8: Avoid a sloppy or extreme appearance in professional settings

© Jupiterimages Corporation

© Jupiterimages Corporation

TABLE A-4: Practicing good grooming and hygiene do's and don'ts

guideline	do	don't
Bathe every day	• Take a shower or bath every day • Choose lightly scented or unscented products	• **Don't** use scented soaps and shampoos • **Don't** forget to bathe after physical activities
Groom your hair	• If you are male, shave or trim your facial hair at least once a day • Shampoo often enough to keep your hair looking and smelling clean • Brush or comb your hair at the beginning of the day and as necessary after that	• **Don't** use shampoos or conditioners with harsh chemicals • **Don't** choose hair styles that are not appropriate for your company or position
Keep your breath fresh	• Brush your teeth regularly • Use mouthwash and mints to keep your breath fresh after brushing	**Don't** forget to brush your teeth, rinse your mouth, or use breath mints after eating or drinking anything with an odor

UNIT
A
Professionalism

Interacting with Others

Part of professional life involves meeting and interacting with other people. Your greeting helps you make a positive first impression on new acquaintances. It also sends a signal about your mood and disposition to people who you know well. A proper greeting is a social skill that comes naturally for some people but can be difficult for others. Fortunately, anyone can learn and develop this ability. Table A-5 summarizes the do's and don'ts of interacting with others. Tia emphasizes that professional interactions lead to success at Quest Specialty Travel. You decide to develop a training session on interacting with others.

ESSENTIAL ELEMENTS

1. **Develop and practice a short elevator speech**

   You often meet people when you least expect it. By preparing and practicing a basic introduction about yourself (sometimes called an **elevator speech** because it takes as long as an elevator ride with a colleague) you'll feel more confident when meeting someone unexpectedly. Your standard introduction should include your name and information about your company, position, and what you do. Then tailor your introduction to match the circumstances and person you are meeting.

2. **Stand up when greeting someone**

   Standing and facing the person you are meeting is a basic rule of etiquette that is often overlooked. Remaining seated when meeting someone can be interpreted by the other person as disrespect. If it is difficult for you to rise (when you are holding something on your lap or using a wheelchair, for example), acknowledge it and ask to be excused for not standing.

3. **Smile and make eye contact**

   Your facial expressions communicate more than your words. Smiling shows you are pleased to meet the other person, regardless of what you may be thinking. Looking companions in the eye while you chat indicates you are interested in them and what they have to say. Glancing elsewhere when you greet and chat with someone suggests that you have other things on your mind.

> **QUICK TIP**
> When you are wearing a name tag, wear it high on the right shoulder so it remains visible as you shake hands.

4. **Offer to shake hands**

   Shaking hands is an important custom in professional greetings. Don't wait for the other person to introduce themselves. Take the initiative and offer your hand as you start your introduction. Doing so is a strong sign of confidence and puts the other person at ease. Professional handshakes should be firm, but not overly aggressive. Your handshake should last for about three seconds before releasing your grip. See Figure A-9.

5. **Be prepared to meet people**

   Prepare for interactions at meetings, social gatherings, or other events. Identify the people you want to meet, memorize their names, and try to find out something about them in advance. Knowing a little about their company, department, or projects gives you information to chat about and makes the exchange more interesting. Other suitable topics for casual conversation include current events, sports, and popular culture.

YOU TRY IT

1. **Use a word processor such as Microsoft Office Word to open the file A-5.doc provided with your Data Files, and save it as Interacting.doc in the location where you store your Data Files**
2. **Read the contents of Interacting.doc, which describe a business encounter**
3. **Complete the table in the document to evaluate the professional etiquette of the people involved**
4. **Save and close Interacting.doc, then submit it to your instructor as requested**

FIGURE A-9: Shake hands when meeting someone

© Jupiterimages Corporation

TABLE A-5: Interacting with others do's and don'ts

guideline	do	don't
Develop an elevator speech	• Prepare a basic introduction about yourself • Tailor your introduction to include details important or interesting to the person you are meeting	**Don't** make your introduction too detailed
Greet people	• Greet people with a smile and customary expression such as "Good morning" • Shake hands firmly when meeting someone for the first time • Smile and make eye contact as you greet someone • Introduce yourself when you meet someone for the first time	• **Don't** ignore someone you don't know when you enter a room • **Don't** shake hands too weakly or too strongly • **Don't** remain seated when introducing yourself to someone
Be prepared to meet people	• Before attending an event, identify the people you want to meet • Learn about the people you want to meet	**Don't** avoid meeting others; professional events are ideal for networking

Preparing a memorable elevator speech

An elevator speech is a sentence or two that introduces you to someone else during the length of an elevator ride, which is about 15–30 seconds. Basically, an elevator speech describes what you do and how it can benefit your listeners. For example, if you work in the travel industry and are meeting potential clients, you might say, "I'm Tia Patterson, and I help travelers design the trip of their lifetime." If you are introducing yourself to a corporate customer, you might say "I'm Tia Patterson, and I work with companies who want to provide travel incentives that encourage sales and business growth." As in both examples, after you introduce yourself by name, explain what you do in terms that your listener will find interesting. Use a short, memorable phrase that stimulates interest. Speak with a firm, confident voice. If you sense that your listener is interested, be prepared to exchange business cards or offer to make contact through a phone call or e-mail message.

UNIT A
Professionalism

ESSENTIAL ELEMENTS

Improving Your Speech

People use all of their senses to learn about others they meet. Besides judging you on your physical appearance, people evaluate how you speak. Your choice of words, pronunciation, tone of voice, and other characteristics reveal your background, level of education, and where you are from. Poor speech habits can make you sound too informal and interfere with the image you want to portray. Table A-6 lists the do's and don'ts for improving your speech. After outlining a training session on interacting with others, you also decide to develop a session on improving speaking habits.

1. **Record yourself**
   You cannot improve your speech habits until you know how you sound to others. Use a recording device or microphone on your computer to record yourself having a casual conversation with someone. (Be sure to ask their permission first.) See Figure A-10. Speak in a normal tone of voice and style. Because it might take several minutes before you relax and speak normally, record 15–20 minutes of conversation. Review this objectively, and identify areas that might need improvement.

QUICK TIP
Practicing your diction helps your pronunciation in conversation and when making presentations.

2. **Practice reading aloud**
   Diction is the degree of clarity and proper pronunciation in your speech. You can improve your diction by regularly reading aloud a newspaper, novel, or other written material. A book of tongue-twisters will give you an intense workout. Slow down your pronunciation of long and complex words. As you feel more comfortable, gradually increase your rate of speaking.

QUICK TIP
Examples of assimilation include "I dunno," "gonna," "probly," and "coulda."

3. **Avoid assimilation**
   People frequently blend sounds together, or **assimilate**, when they speak. This is normal and allows them to speak more quickly and with less effort. However, blended words are difficult to understand and make the speaker sound less articulate.

4. **Mimic the news anchors**
   If English is not your first language, you can improve your speech by listening to professional speakers. Tune into television or radio news programs and imitate the anchors as they talk. Mimic their accent, pronunciation, and speaking patterns.

QUICK TIP
Replace vague terms such as "things" and "whatever" with words that express what you want to say.

5. **Slow down**
   Awkward speech habits are more obvious when you speak quickly. Make an effort to consciously slow down when speaking in a professional setting such as a meeting, interview, or conversation with your manager. Slowing your speech can also help improve your pronunciation if you have a strong regional accent.

6. **Increase your vocabulary**
   Your choice of words is as important as how you say them. Having a rich vocabulary allows you to speak more fluently and expressively. Search the Internet for *SAT words* or *GRE words* for vocabulary word suggestions. See Figure A-11, which shows the beginning of a list of vocabulary words at *www.freevocabulary.com*. Write the words on note cards and set a goal to learn two or three new words each day. This will increase your vocabulary by 500–1000 words each year and help improve your speaking ability.

YOU TRY IT

1. **Use a word processor such as Microsoft Office Word to open the file A-6.doc provided with your Data Files, and save it as Speech.doc in the location where you store your Data Files**
2. **Read the contents of Speech.doc, which describe a business conversation**
3. **List the pros and cons of the employee's speech habits**
4. **Save and close Speech.doc, then submit it to your instructor as requested**

FIGURE A-10: Practice and record how you speak

© Jupiterimages Corporation

FIGURE A-11: Search for Web sites listing vocabulary words

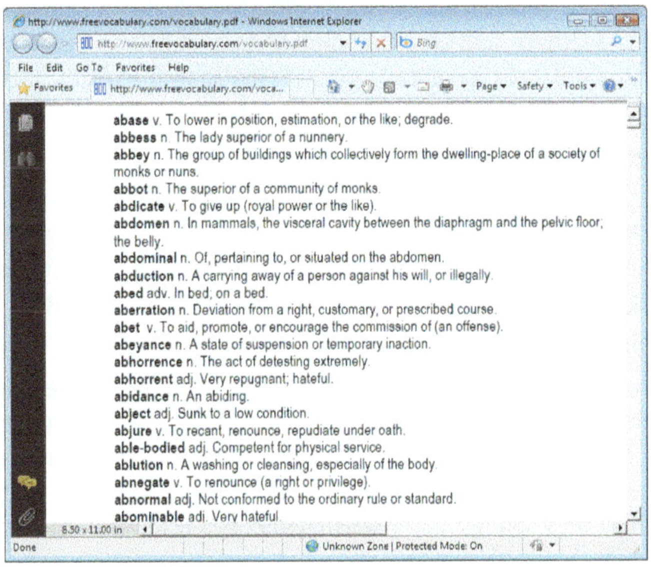

freevocabulary.com

TABLE A-6: Improving your speech do's and don'ts

guideline	do	don't
Record yourself	• Use a recording device or microphone on your computer to record yourself having a casual conversation • Ask for your companion's permission before recording • Record your normal voice tone and style for 15–20 minutes • Evaluate your speech objectively, and look for areas to improve	**Don't** think you can improve your speech habits without knowing how you sound to others
Practice your speech	• Read aloud to improve your diction, which is the clarity and proper pronunciation of words • Slow down your pronunciation of a complex word until it becomes natural to you • Listen to and mimic professional speakers such as news anchors	• **Don't** practice your diction by reading aloud too quickly • **Don't** assimilate, or blend sounds together when you speak • **Don't** speak quickly, especially in a professional setting
Increase your vocabulary	• Develop a rich vocabulary so you can speak fluently and expressively • Search the Internet for vocabulary lists	**Don't** rely on vague terms such as "things" and "whatever"—learn the right words to express what you want to say

UNIT
A
Professionalism

Cleaning Up Your Online Persona

The Internet, Web, and e-mail are standard tools in your working and personal life. Millions of people use social networking sites, post comments on blogs and bulletin boards, and maintain personal Web pages. Collectively, the publicly searchable information available about you makes up your **online persona**. Your online persona often makes an impression on people before you meet them. In a recent survey by executive search firm ExecuNet, 77 of 100 recruiters said they use search engines to check out job candidates. A growing number of employers now use the Internet to check up on their employees. Quest Specialty Travel employs many recent graduates, and Tia wants to make sure their online profiles are professional and appropriate. You decide to research how to clean up online personas.

ESSENTIAL ELEMENTS

QUICK TIP
Using several search engines gives you a more complete picture of your online persona.

1. **Search for yourself**
   Get in the habit of researching yourself online to evaluate the search results. Use Google and other search engines to search for yourself using your full name, common nicknames, and initials (as in Tia Patterson and T. Patterson). Look for other people with the same or similar names who could easily be confused with you. Note any material that others might consider as negative.

QUICK TIP
You can write to Google and other search engines to ask them not to index a page that contains damaging information.

2. **Eliminate negative material**
   Some of the content on the Internet cannot be completely eliminated, but you can control some material. Revise your home page and profiles you have on social networking, dating, and similar sites. Remove controversial photos, comments, blog entries, and links. If you find negative content on a site you do not control, send a polite letter to the site owner and ask them to remove it.

3. **Dilute what you cannot remove**
   If you find potentially damaging material that you cannot remove, dilute it instead by adding more positive content. Create as much positive content as you can, and submit it to a variety of sites, including blog entries, product reviews, advice, and comments in public bulletin boards. For example, enter a positive book review on a bookseller's Web site. Include your name on all of your submissions. Search engines prefer new content and list it first in the search results, before any links to negative content.

4. **Use privacy settings**
   You can share personal information with your friends but not with everyone on the Internet. Most social networking sites include privacy controls, though the default setting might make all of your information public. Change the settings to limit how much casual visitors can see and access. See Figure A-12. Periodically review the people with whom you are sharing private information.

QUICK TIP
Remember that your anonymous persona should never be used for fraudulent purposes or to deceive someone.

5. **Create an anonymous persona**
   If you like to participate and post on controversial sites, consider creating an anonymous persona. It is common practice to use an assumed name, or handle, when posting or responding on blogs and bulletin boards. For example, you could be SoccerFan09 on a sports blog. Create an e-mail address on one of the free e-mail services such as Gmail or Yahoo Mail, and use it for nonbusiness correspondence.

YOU TRY IT

1. Use a word processor such as Microsoft Office Word to open the file A-7.doc provided with your Data Files, and save it as Persona.doc in the location where you store your Data Files
2. Read the contents of Persona.doc, which describe a job hunter's online persona
3. Suggest specific ways for the job hunter to improve her online persona
4. Save and close Persona.doc, then submit it to your instructor as requested

FIGURE A-12: Privacy settings for Facebook and LinkedIn

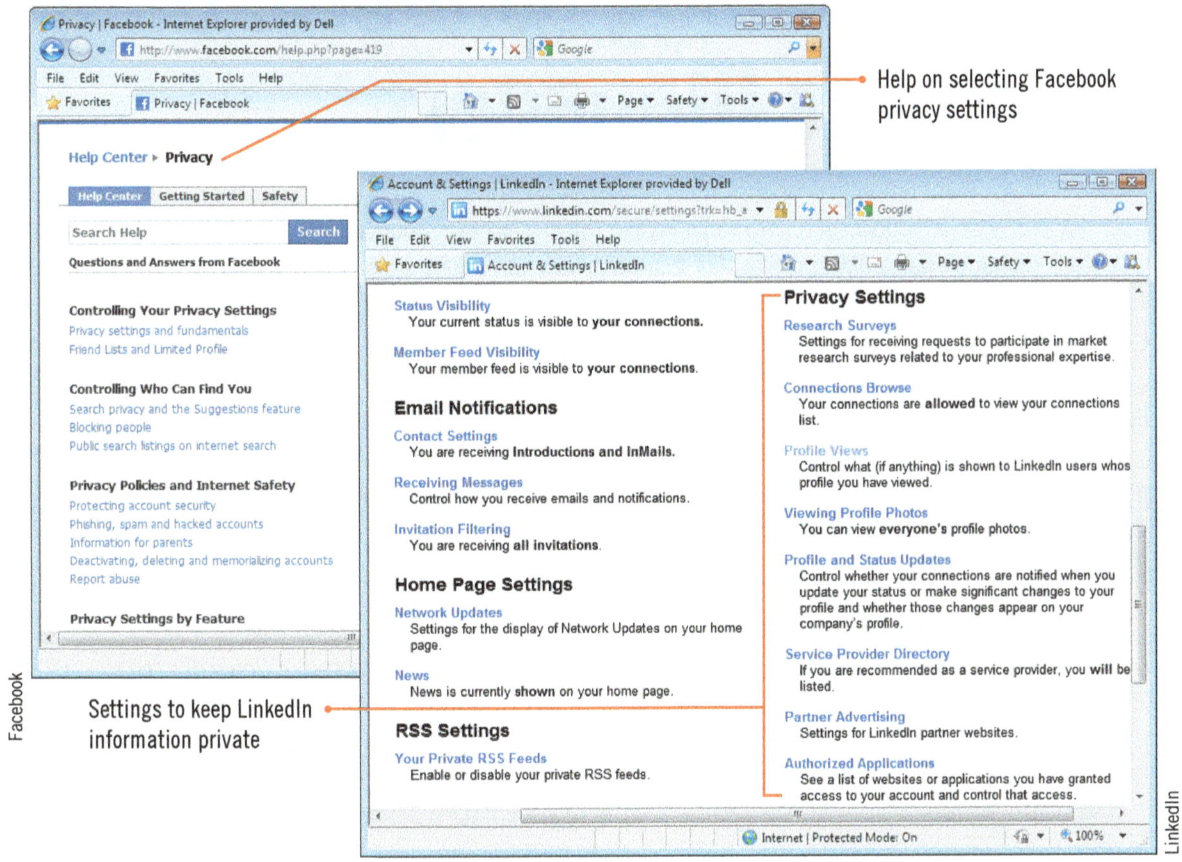

Developing your online brand

According to the *Boston Globe*, "A positive online persona is so crucial to career success these days that even invisibility can be a drawback." Besides taking steps to prevent and remove inappropriate photos and other content from Web sites, you should also take time to create a positive personal brand, which is basically your public image. "If you don't brand yourself, Google will brand you," says Sherry Beck Paprocki, co-author of *The Complete Idiot's Guide to Branding Yourself.* Your goal is to control the information potential employers or customers find when they use a search engine to learn more about you. Alina Tugend of the *New York Times* offers the following advice: establish a presence on a site such as LinkedIn, Facebook, or Twitter. Then join a few other sites that focus on your field or professional interests. Veronica Fielding, president of Digital Brand Expressions, suggests, "You want to find groups—alumni, former employees of your last jobs, trade groups." Join the groups, and then contribute to discussions when you have an insight or thoughtful comment. That way, Fielding says, "when people are thinking about filling a job, they think of you."

Sources: Jackson, Maggie, "Your past is lurking online," *Boston Globe*, February 25, 2007; Tugend, Alina, "Putting Yourself Out There on a Shelf to Buy," *New York Times*, March 27, 2009.

UNIT
A
Professionalism

Technology @ Work: Online Profile Managers

If you want employers or customers to find positive information about you, make sure it is available online. You can use tools such as Google Profile (*https://**profiles.google**.com*), and Retaggr (*www.retaggr.com*) to manage your online profiles. For example, you can create a personal Google profile that include links to your online resume or to your organization's Web site. See Figure A-13. When people use the Google search engine to find information about you, your profile appears in the search results. See Figure A-14. The profile displays only information you have added to it. The more details you add to your profile, the higher your page is likely to be ranked in the Google search results for your name and associated keywords, such as the name of your hometown, your job title, or where you work or go to school. Tia has heard about Google Profiles, and wants to know more about it. She suggests you create a profile and then train other QST employees to do the same.

ESSENTIAL ELEMENTS

1. **Set up a Google account**
   Visit *www.google.com/accounts*, and look for a link to create an account. You will need to enter your e-mail address and choose a password. You must have a Google account before you can create a Google profile. Google accounts are a free service.
2. **Create a profile**
   To create an online profile, complete a Web form by entering personal information such as your name, where you grew up, where you currently live, and what you do. You can also provide a short biography, photographs, and describe your interests.
3. **Exchange e-mail and messages**
   In your profile, you can click "Send a message" so that anyone with a Google account can send you e-mail messages without knowing your e-mail address or revealing it to others.
4. **Display links**
   After you create a profile, Google suggests links to other Google products you might enjoy using such as Gmail and Picasa Web Albums. You can then display a link to your photo album, for example, on your Google profile page so that others can review photos from a recent business presentation. The links you select become public, while the links you do not select remain private. You can also enter links to other sites, such as social network profiles and personal Web sites.
5. **Access your profile**
   You can access your profile at *www.google.com/profiles/me*, or when you create content in some Google products such as Google Maps and Book Search. You can also send this URL to friends and family members.

YOU TRY IT

1. **Open a Web browser such as Microsoft Internet Explorer or Mozilla Firefox, and go to the Google Profiles Web site at *www.google.com/profiles***
2. **Follow the steps to create a Google account, if necessary, and then to create a profile**
3. **Press the Print Screen key to take a screen shot of your profile page, open a word-processing program such as Microsoft Word, press Ctrl+V to paste the screen shot in a new document, and then send the document to your instructor**

FIGURE A-13: Creating a Google profile

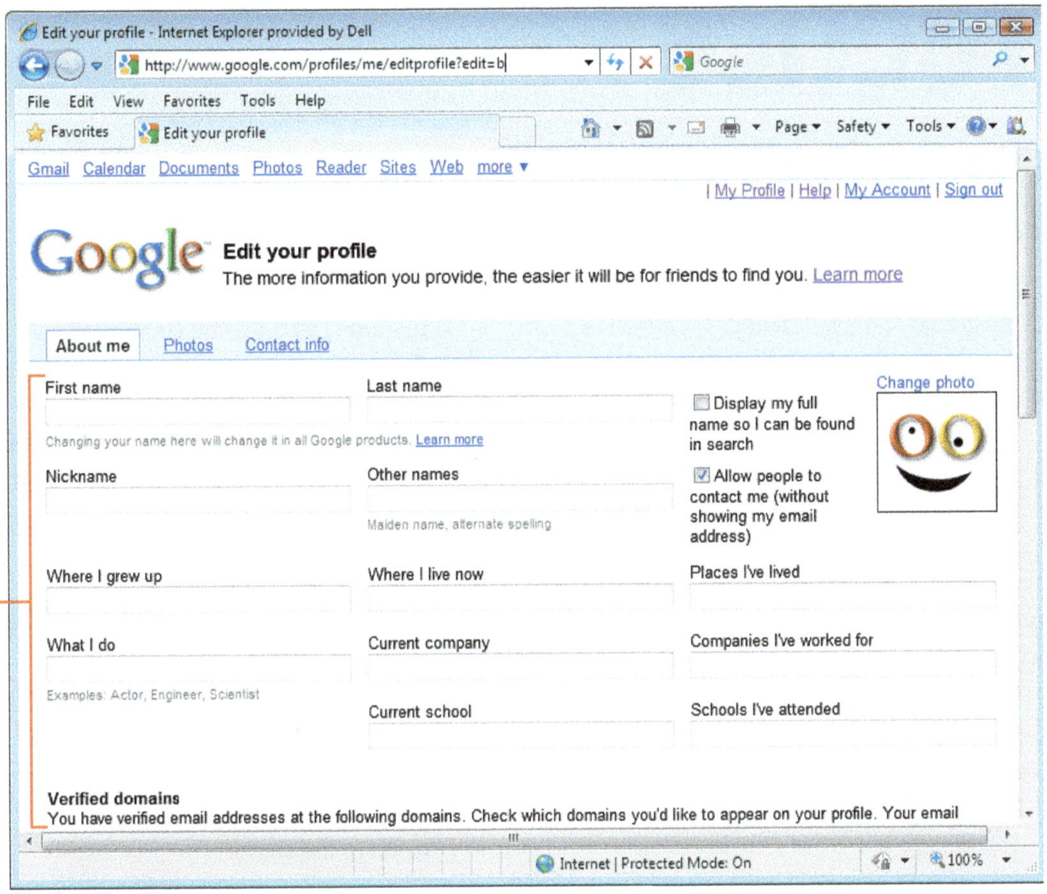

Enter information you want others to know about you

Google

FIGURE A-14: Sample Google profile

Profile page

Google search results

Google

Professionalism

Practice

SOFT SKILLS REVIEW

Manage your image.

1. **A classic piece of career advice is to dress for:**
   - **a.** the last position you held
   - **b.** the next position you are seeking
   - **c.** formal settings and circumstances
   - **d.** an easy transition to your private life
2. **Why should you dress appropriately for your position, company, and occasion?**
   - **a.** To help develop your online brand
   - **b.** Your company requires you to do so
   - **c.** The way you dress helps you analyze reports
   - **d.** The way you dress affects your confidence and others' impressions of you

Dress appropriately.

1. **In previous generations, dress codes dictated that professionals wear suits, jackets, dresses, long-sleeved shirts, ties, and leather shoes, a style known as:**
   - **a.** international standard business attire
   - **b.** international business machines
   - **c.** business casual
   - **d.** business formal
2. **Norms for professional dress often vary by:**
   - **a.** location
   - **b.** department
   - **c.** industry
   - **d.** all of the above

Meet business casual standards.

1. **If your organization defines its dress code as business casual, that means:**
   - **a.** you can wear the same clothes you wear at home
   - **b.** you never need to wear a suit
   - **c.** you should wear clothes less formal than a traditional suit and tie, yet dressier than jeans and a t-shirt
   - **d.** you should wear a jacket or blazer, even if it is wrinkled or ripped
2. **Which of the following *is not* a common element of business casual attire?**
   - **a.** Collared shirt
   - **b.** Athletic t-shirt
   - **c.** Comfortable yet dressy shoes
   - **d.** Slacks

Maintain a professional wardrobe.

1. **What can you do to keep your clothing pressed and neat?**
   - **a.** Remove clothes from the dryer promptly
   - **b.** Spray on liquid sizing before ironing
   - **c.** Iron and hang clothes
   - **d.** All of the above
2. **Which of the following *is not* a way to maintain a professional wardrobe?**
   - **a.** Wash colored and white clothes together
   - **b.** Hand wash and dry-clean clothes as necessary
   - **c.** Iron and hang clothes
   - **d.** Polish your shoes

Practice good grooming and hygiene.

1. **The practice of maintaining cleanliness and health is called:**
   - **a.** business casual
   - **b.** your persona
   - **c.** personal hygiene
   - **d.** business hygiene
2. **How often should you shampoo and condition your hair?**
   - **a.** Once a day
   - **b.** Twice a day
   - **c.** Often enough to keep your hair looking and smelling clean
   - **d.** Rarely so your scalp does not dry out

Interact with others.

1. **You can make a good first impression by:**
   - **a.** shaking hands
   - **b.** telling an off-color joke
   - **c.** remaining seated
   - **d.** answering your cell phone
2. **An elevator speech is:**
   - **a.** a speech you rehearse by yourself in an elevator
   - **b.** a short, basic introduction to yourself
   - **c.** an inspirational speech that "lifts you up"
   - **d.** the story of your life

Improve your speech.

1. **The degree of clarity and proper pronunciation in your speech is called:**
   - **a.** denotation
   - **b.** diction
   - **c.** tongue-twisting
   - **d.** pitch
2. **Why should you aim to have a rich vocabulary?**
   - **a.** To make people look up words in the dictionary
   - **b.** It is part of a business casual outlook
   - **c.** It allows you to speak fluently and expressively
   - **d.** It improves your diction

Clean up your online persona.

1. **Your online persona is:**
   - **a.** separate from your professional image
   - **b.** how you interact with colleagues, clients, and visitors
   - **c.** how you are represented on social networking sites and other online locations
   - **d.** an electronic version of your dress code
2. **Which of the following is *not* a way to advertise your strengths online?**
   - **a.** Create a personal Web site
   - **b.** Emphasize strengths on your social network site
   - **c.** Leave personal photos on your social network site
   - **d.** Create a Google profile

Technology @ work: Online profile managers

1. **Why should you use tools such as Google Profile to manage your online profile?**
   - **a.** To make sure employers and customers find positive information about you
   - **b.** To protect against identity theft
   - **c.** To change your online identity
   - **d.** All of the above
2. **If you have a Google Profile, what happens when people use the Google search engine to find information about you?**
   - **a.** Sites with embarrassing information do not appear in the results
   - **b.** Your profile appears in the search results
   - **c.** You can schedule a group meeting
   - **d.** Visitors can view photos in your private photo album

▼ CRITICAL THINKING QUESTIONS

1. **This unit provides guidelines for creating a professional image. How important are appearances in the business world? Are they more important than professional ethics?**
2. **As mentioned in the introduction to this unit, studies suggest that most people form impressions about a new acquaintance within the first minute or two of interaction. Are you one of the majority who form impressions quickly? Have you had to reconsider your impression later, after getting to know someone?**
3. **What do you consider acceptable attire for your chosen field? Be specific about acceptable articles of clothing. How did you determine which clothes are acceptable and which are not?**
4. **Suppose you are working closely with a colleague, and notice that he needs to improve one of the guidelines covered in this lesson, such as maintaining a professional wardrobe or improving speech habits. How would you handle this situation?**
5. **Do you think it is fair and ethical for employers and customers to search for information about you online? Why or why not?**

▼ INDEPENDENT CHALLENGE 1

Dale and Greg Coffman are brothers who recently started a business called Coffman Bakery in Barrington, Illinois. They provide baked goods such as bread, rolls, pastries, cakes, tortes, pies, and cookies to grocery stores in northern Illinois. Dale and Greg hired you as a part-time salesperson. Your duties are to meet customers at their stores or in your office and sell Coffman Bakery products. Dale and Greg want to develop a business casual dress code for you and the other salespeople, and have created a list of notes on the dress code they want to establish. See Figure A-15.

FIGURE A-15

Business Casual Dress Code

Coffman Bakery has a business casual dress code so our employees can work comfortably in the bakery and project a professional image for our customers, potential employees, and community visitors.

Acceptable clothing for men:
Acceptable clothing for women:
Acceptable clothing for men or women:
Unacceptable clothing for men and women:

- Suit, including a matching jacket and skirt
- Dresses, skirts, skirts with jackets, dressy two-piece knit suits or sets, and skirts that are split at or below the knee are acceptable
- Dress and skirt length should be at a length at which you can sit comfortably in public
- Tasteful, professional scarves, belts, and jewelry
- Suit, including a matching jacket and pants and a coordinated tie
- Slacks including cotton khakis or synthetic material pants, wool pants, flannel pants, and pants that match a suit jacket
- Athletic shoes, tennis shoes, thongs, flip-flops, slippers, or other casual shoes with an open toe

a. Use word-processing software such as Microsoft Office Word to open the file **A-8.doc** provided with your Data Files, and save it as **Dress Code.doc** in the location where you store your Data Files.

b. Rearrange and revise the list of acceptable and unacceptable clothing in Dress Code.doc so it meets the standards of business casual attire.

c. Submit the document to your instructor as requested.

▼ INDEPENDENT CHALLENGE 2

You work with Louise Harper, the owner of Harmony Day Spa in Silver Spring, Maryland. As the front desk manager, you develop guidelines for the hair stylists and other staff to follow when working at the spa. Louise asks you to address customer interactions, including grooming, hygiene, and greetings, in a short document. You start by outlining the topics you plan to cover, as shown in Figure A-16. Louise wants to emphasize that employees should choose a hair style that reflects the upscale image of the spa.

FIGURE A-16

Outline for Customer Interaction Guidelines

- **Grooming**
  Hair
  Makeup
- **Hygiene**
  Shower/bath
  Breath
  Feet
- **Greetings**
  Initial greeting
  Eye contact
  Shake hands
  Introduce yourself

a. Use word-processing software such as Microsoft Office Word to open the file **A-9.doc** provided with your Data Files, and save it as **Customer Interactions.doc** in the location where you store your Data Files.
b. Expand the outline shown in Figure A-16 into a detailed list of guidelines suitable for the staff of the Harmony Day Spa.
c. Submit the document to your instructor as requested.

▼ REAL LIFE INDEPENDENT CHALLENGE

You are preparing for a job search and want to enhance your image so it is as appealing as possible to a potential employer. Start by making sure your online persona is professional and appealing.

a. Using two or three search engines (such as Google, Bing, and Yahoo), look up your name online. Do you find anything potentially embarrassing or unprofessional? If so, contact the sites where you found the information and ask to have it removed.
b. Review your social networking site profiles. Have you posted comments, stories, or photographs on social networking sites such as Facebook or MySpace that a prospective employer might object to? Have friends posted unprofessional information that could be associated with you? If so, remove the content. For example, if you find a group photo that includes your image, you might be able to remove the photo by clicking a "remove" link next to your name.
c. Also review your personal Web site or blog, if you have one. If you have written about topics that an employer might find unprofessional, remove those as well.
d. If you don't have an online persona, create one suitable for your chosen field using a tool such as Google Profile.
e. Visit a few Web sites for products you use, such as books or electronic devices, find a product you like, and then click a button or link to write a positive review.

▼ TEAM CHALLENGE

You are working for Clean Fields, Inc., a company in Little Rock, Arkansas specializing in recovering land that has been contaminated or polluted. You are part of a project team working to study a site near Hot Springs and recommend whether it can be used for building a shopping center. Your team is preparing to meet with your client in Hot Springs, and your manager, Larry Owens, suggests that you work on your social interaction and speech skills. (If you are working online and have a microphone attached to your computer, use the microphone to record your speech, and then send the sound file to your partner.)

a. Work as a team to discuss how you will greet, interact with, and speak to your client, a real-estate developer.
b. Work with a partner to identify one area in your interactions or speech that you would like to improve. Discuss how you can improve in this area.
c. Play the role of the client, and let your partner play the role of a member of Clean Fields. Greet each other, briefly discuss the purpose of the meeting, and then plan your next action.
d. Switch roles and complete the same tasks: greet each other, briefly discuss the purpose of the meeting, and then plan your next action.
e. Working again as a team, let each person offer one suggestion for improving your interactions or speech habits.

▼ BE THE CRITIC

You have been working for a small business called Gateway Events, which organizes events for groups, such as conferences, grand openings, and trade shows. As a member of the team that trains new employees, you often give advice about developing a professional image, especially when meeting with clients. Figure A-17 shows a new employee on his first day on the job as an event planner at Gateway Events. Analyze the impression the new employee makes, and then note details about his presentation that are not professional or appropriate. Send a list of these details to your instructor.

FIGURE A-17

© Jupiterimages Corporation

UNIT
B
Professionalism

Developing a Professional Work Ethic

Files You Will Need:
B-1.doc
B-2.doc
B-3.doc
B-4.doc
B-5.doc
B-6.doc
B-7.doc
B-8.doc

When a company hires you and agrees to pay a particular wage or salary, they expect your best efforts in return. This is particularly true when you are hired in a professional role or position. The effort, attitude, and commitment that you bring to your job are sometimes referred to as your work ethic. Employees that demonstrate a professional work ethic are more likely to be given more responsibility, better compensation, and promotions. In this unit, you will learn about the principles of a professional work ethic and explore how to develop one. Tia Patterson is the director of the Quest Specialty Travel (QST) branch in New York City, and you assist her in hiring and training staff members. Tia recently hired a few recent graduates to work as travel professionals, and knows their success depends on their work ethic and commitment to the company and its clients. She is organizing a few days of orientation for these new employees and asks you to help her during the orientation.

OBJECTIVES

- Demonstrate your work ethic and commitment
- Be dependable and reliable
- Manage your time
- Manage stress
- Maintain a professional workspace
- Take advantage of professional opportunities
- Earn recognition

UNIT B
Professionalism

Demonstrating Your Work Ethic and Commitment

Professionals differ from laborers in several ways, such as having more control over schedules, working with less direct supervision, and developing greater variety in their responsibilities over time. In exchange for this trust, professional employees are expected to demonstrate a good **work ethic**. This is a complex term that includes personal characteristics such as dependability, initiative, effort, responsibility, integrity, and punctuality. Your work ethic is a reflection of how you feel about and do your job. Without a good personal work ethic, your performance will typically fall short of what your employer and colleagues expect of you. Tia Patterson suggests you prepare for the first orientation session by reviewing the basics of developing a work ethic and committing to a job.

DETAILS

If you have a strong work ethic and job commitment, you demonstrate it in the following ways:

> **QUICK TIP**
> In surveys, employers indicate that a strong work ethic is one of a job candidate's top-five traits.

- **Do the right thing**
  Demonstrate integrity in both your personal and professional dealings. This means you always tell the truth and make appropriate choices. Never engage in behavior that others might consider sneaky, underhanded, or dishonest. Your reputation is the foundation of your work ethic.
- **Exceed expectations**
  Exceed your manager's expectations by promising less and delivering more. A surprise is a gap between what you expect and what you find or receive, and you want to surprise your manager in a positive way, not negatively. Do more than your managers, colleagues, and customers expect.
- **Assist others as part of your job**
  Do not fall into the trap of limiting what you will and will not do. Most organizations have more tasks that need to be performed than people to perform them. If you think you can help another person—whether colleague, customer, or vendor—pitch in and make yourself useful. Helping others not only supports your organization and coworkers, but builds your image as a team player. See Figure B-1.

> **QUICK TIP**
> Even a sole proprietor has customers who count on him or her to deliver products or services.

- **Remember that others are depending on you**
  Unless you are a sole proprietor in a one-person business, you work with others to accomplish tasks and projects. No matter what your role, others will depend on you to meet your responsibilities. When you are late, forgetful, or overcommitted, the consequences affect you and others. See Figure B-2. Assign the highest priority to your shared commitments.
- **Find your inner motivation**
  Physical things such as a private office and high salary are important parts of any job, but they are not enough to keep most people motivated. Over time, you will be more committed to an organization you are interested in and feel good about. Focus on what you enjoy in your job responsibilities, environment, and others that you work with. If you work full-time, you spend more than 2,000 hours a year working. You will be more successful if you are motivated to work each day.

FIGURE B-1: Helping others builds your image as a team player

© Jupiterimages Corporation

FIGURE B-2: Remember that others are depending on you

© Jupiterimages Corporation

Want to be an entrepreneur? Develop a strong work ethic

An **entrepreneur** is someone who starts a new business, often risking their own investments of time and money. Those who succeed inevitably do so because of their work ethic—their "job commitment and achievement, of short-term pain for long-term gain," as Amy McCourtney and Dennis Engels define it in *Career Development Quarterly*.

One example of an entrepreneur with a strong work ethic is Ingvar Kamprad, founder of the Swedish home-furnishings retailer IKEA. According to his biography in About.com, Kamprad's father rewarded him for succeeding in his studies when he was seventeen, and he used that money to start a business that grew into IKEA. Adhering to his principles of self-sufficiency, frugality, and designing affordable, quality furniture, Kamprad instilled his work ethic in his employees and quickly built his business into a powerhouse. *Forbes* magazine reports that IKEA now sells "9,500 items in 36 countries; prints catalog in 27 languages. [Its] revenues were up 7% to $27.4 billion in fiscal year 2008."

Another example of an entrepreneur who started from scratch is Debbi Fields, founder of Mrs. Fields Cookies, a $450 million company she started in 1977. When she was 20 years old, Fields developed a popular chocolate-chip cookie recipe and decided to open a chocolate-chip cookie bakeshop. Though such a store was considered a risky venture at the time, Fields pursued her dream of providing high-quality cookies and developing loyal customers. Today, Mrs. Fields Cookies has more than 600 stores in the U.S. and 10 other countries. Obviously, none of this would be possible without her "job commitment and achievement, of short-term pain for long-term gain."

Sources: Allen, Scott, "Ingvar Kamprad—IKEA Founder and One of the World's Richest Men," entrepreneurs.about.com, accessed October 15, 2009; McCourtney, Amy and Engels, Dennis, "Revisiting the Work Ethic in America," *Career Development Quarterly*, December 2003; Staff, "About Mrs. Fields," *www.debbifields.com*, accessed October 15, 2009; Staff, "The World's Richest People: Ingvar Kamprad," *www.forbes.com*, accessed October 15, 2009.

UNIT
B
Professionalism

Being Dependable and Reliable

Your career will blossom when others in your organization recognize you as dependable and reliable. **Dependable** employees demonstrate through their reliability, honesty, and trustworthiness that they can be counted on to deliver as promised. Someone who is **reliable** can perform a job under routine circumstances and act responsibly when the unexpected occurs. When you are dependable, you are available and ready to provide your professional service when it is expected or needed. Successful leaders often surround themselves with dependable people and are more likely to offer opportunities to those they can trust and rely on. Table B-1 lists the do's and don'ts of being dependable and reliable. After exploring strong work ethics and committing to a job in your orientation session, you have time to discuss being dependable and reliable.

ESSENTIAL ELEMENTS

QUICK TIP
You can use a Web calendar from anywhere if you have a web browser.

1. **Keep track of your commitments**
   In a hectic work environment, you need a personal information manager or calendar tool to remind you of commitments and obligations. Some people like to use a portable digital assistant with appropriate software, such as a smartphone. See Figure B-3. Others are more comfortable with a small calendar booklet or time-management system. Find and use an approach that works for you.
2. **Manage expectations**
   If your job expectations differ from your manager's, you might miss the credit you deserve when doing a good job. If a task or project turns out to require more than you planned, your performance will not be satisfactory. When discussing a job assignment, be sure to clarify your role and responsibility with your manager. Develop common expectations when you accept new tasks.
3. **Practice consistent attendance**
   Because other people in your organization expect you to be available when they need assistance, practice good attendance habits. Do not miss work without having an acceptable reason. Plan your vacations and discuss the details with your manager. Be punctual to work each day, to meetings, and other scheduled events. Tardiness is an unprofessional habit that is disrespectful of others.

QUICK TIP
Arriving extremely early provides little additional benefit.

4. **Arrive early**
   Arriving to work early each morning gives you undisturbed time every day, and lets others know that you are a committed employee. Stay through the end of the work day and later if your team is working on an important project or has a deadline looming. Some career advisors suggest that you arrive earlier and stay later than your boss. This can be especially effective at organizations where raises and promotions are competitive.

YOU TRY IT

1. **Use a word processor such as Microsoft Office Word to open the file B-1.doc provided with your Data Files, and save it as Dependable.doc in the location where you store your Data Files**
2. **Read the contents of Dependable.doc, which describe a business situation**
3. **Use the guidelines in this lesson to list how the employee could be more dependable and reliable**
4. **Save and close Dependable.doc, then submit it to your instructor as requested**

FIGURE B-3: Track commitments with a planning tool

© Jupiterimages Corporation

© Jupiterimages Corporation

TABLE B-1: Being dependable and reliable do's and don'ts

guideline	do	don't
Track commitments	• Use a personal information manager or calendar tool • Consider a portable digital assistant or smartphone • Keep a paper calendar or booklet up to date	**Don't** rely on your memory to meet your commitments
Manage expectations	• Understand your manager's expectations of you • Discuss the expectations of each job assignment • Communicate directly with your manager as soon as possible after an unexpected event	• **Don't** assume your job responsibilities without discussing them with your manager • **Don't** let conflicting expectations result in poor job performance • **Don't** send an e-mail message to explain an unexpected circumstance that affects your job
Practice consistent attendance	• Attend work, meetings, conferences, and other events as promised • Plan vacations and discuss the details about your departure and return times • Be punctual to scheduled events	• **Don't** miss work without having an acceptable reason • **Don't** explain absences after the fact
Arrive early	• Arrive to work before most other employees do • Stay through to the end of each workday • Be prepared to work late if your project or team requires it	• **Don't** arrive late without notifying someone in advance • **Don't** start packing up to leave well before the stated closing time

Advice from a workplace guru

Workplace expert Stephen Viscusi, author of *Bulletproof Your Job*, offers advice about keeping a job and building a successful career. "Bulletproofing your job is almost entirely about the relationship you have with your boss. If your boss knows you, likes you, has a good impression of you, you're much less likely to be fired than someone who doesn't enjoy that relationship with the boss." One strategy he recommends is simply being visible—making sure your boss knows you are contributing to the success of the company. According to Viscusi, one way to be visible is to "Arrive early and stay late . . . You only have to arrive five minutes earlier and stay five minutes later than your boss to give him the impression that you're always there. Also, not taking long lunches or personal days . . . If you're not there, you're easy to fire. Out of sight, out of mind." Another strategy Viscusi suggests is being easy by making your boss's job easier. "Being dependable," he explains, "is an old-school way to bulletproof yourself. Do what you say you're going to do every single time. No excuses, no buck passing, no dog ate your homework, no computer crashes. If your boss knows without a doubt that he can depend on you, day-to-day as well as in an emergency, you will get a pass on the pink slip."

Source: Viscusi, Stephen, "Bulletproof Your Job," *www.huffingtonpost.com*, posted October 2, 2008.

Professionalism

UNIT B

Professionalism

Managing Your Time

Time is one of your most valuable resources, one you need to manage effectively. Part of cultivating an effective work ethic includes developing time-management skills. **Time management** is a set of tools and techniques you can use to schedule your time and accomplish particular tasks, goals, and projects. Time management involves planning, scheduling, ranking, and monitoring how you use your time. Table B-2 lists the do's and don'ts of managing your time. Tia has noticed that many of the new hires need tips on managing their time in the busy New York office. You offer to discuss time management skills during the next orientation session.

ESSENTIAL ELEMENTS

1. **Identify time-wasting activities**
   Most people have time-wasting habits such as browsing the Web, checking e-mail repeatedly, and socializing electronically or in person. These habits take time away from more productive tasks. Make a log of how you spend your time for a week or so. Note what you are doing every 15–30 minutes. Analyze the results, and calculate how much of each day was productive.

QUICK TIP
Record your top tasks on paper or in a portable device that you can refer to throughout the day.

2. **Plan your day**
   Start each day by listing tasks you want to accomplish. Identify three to five of the most important tasks, and set a deadline for completing them. Include appointments, meetings, e-mail to respond to, and calls to return. See Figure B-4. Setting daily goals helps you accomplish them.

3. **Set priorities**
   Some projects, tasks, and assignments are more urgent or important than others and should be attended to first. As you plan your day, assign a priority to each task on your list. For example, label the high-priority ones as "A," the moderate-priority tasks as "B," and the low-priority entries as "C." Throughout the day, work on the tasks with high priority first.

QUICK TIP
Block distractions only when necessary so other people don't think you are being aloof or inaccessible.

4. **Block distractions**
   Interruptions cause you to lose focus, momentum, and time. Limit distractions so you can manage your time and improve your productivity. Set your e-mail software to check for messages less frequently. Focus on one task at a time. Trying to complete more than one task at a time, or multitasking, actually makes you less productive.

5. **Vary the types of tasks you perform**
   In a typical workday, you look forward to some tasks and want to avoid others. Tasks you want to avoid are probably difficult but as important as other tasks. Budget time each day to work on unpopular or difficult tasks so that you can complete them in stages.

6. **Be flexible**
   Avoid the so-called tyranny of the to-do list. Recognize that you need to complete some tasks that are not on your list. Pace yourself and take occasional breaks. Briefly socializing in the office is part of developing important relationships. Be flexible and change your priorities as necessary.

YOU TRY IT

1. **Use a word processor such as Microsoft Office Word to open the file B-2.doc provided with your Data Files, and save it as Time.doc in the location where you store your Data Files**
2. **Read the contents of Time.doc, which describe a business meeting**
3. **Identify how the employees can better manage their time**
4. **Save and close Time.doc, then submit it to your instructor as requested**

FIGURE B-4: Plan your day

Start each day by listing your priorities, and then refer to them throughout the day

TABLE B-2: Managing your time do's and don'ts

guideline	do	don't
Identify time-wasting activities	• Log how you spend your time for a week or so • Note your activities every 15–30 minutes • Determine how much time you spend on productive tasks each day	• **Don't** waste time by browsing the Web and checking e-mail repeatedly • **Don't** procrastinate by socializing electronically or in person
Plan your day	• Start the day by listing the tasks you want to accomplish • Identify three to five of the most important tasks • Set a deadline for completing the important tasks	**Don't** overlook appointments, meetings, e-mail to respond to, and phone calls to return
Set priorities	• Identify the most urgent and important tasks • Assign a priority to each daily task • Work on the high-priority tasks first	**Don't** label all tasks as high priority; identify the ones that you can complete another day
Block distractions	• Limit distractions by adjusting your e-mail software and phone so they do not interrupt your work • Find a quiet place such as a conference room to complete an important task	• **Don't** let interruptions and other distractions steal too much time • **Don't** work away from your desk too often, or your coworkers will think you are being aloof
Be flexible	• Vary the types of tasks you perform • Perform difficult and enjoyable tasks each day • Budget your time for different types of tasks • Complete some tasks that are not on your to-do list • Take occasional breaks, even to socialize briefly • Change priorities throughout the day or week as necessary	• **Don't** put off completing difficult tasks; work in stages if necessary • **Don't** restrict your activities to items on your to-do list

UNIT
B
Professionalism

Managing Stress

Modern work environments are often filled with deadlines, conflicts, problems, and demands. These can lead to anxiety, stress, and ultimately to exhaustion if not properly managed. **Stress** is your body's response to difficult or dangerous situations. It is designed to help energize you, sharpen your reflexes, and heighten your alertness. In a work setting, stress can help you pay attention, improve your concentration, and boost your energy. However, ongoing stress ceases to be helpful and starts to adversely affect your health, attitude, relationships, and productivity. Table B-3 summarizes the do's and don'ts for managing stress. Tia knows that the upcoming fall and winter season will be particularly busy and stressful. For your next orientation session, she asks you to discuss ways to manage stress.

ESSENTIAL ELEMENTS

1. **Remove yourself from stressful situations**
   When you sense that your stress level is rising, take a break if possible. Put the task off until tomorrow or use your lunch hour to leave the building. Occasional breaks, especially with some physical activity, can help you better manage stress.

2. **Use stress to your advantage**
   When you find yourself in a stressful situation, channel that energy to help you get through it. For example, if you feel anxious before speaking in front of a group, use that nervous energy to help you focus and deliver an enthusiastic presentation.

3. **Eat a snack**
   Studies have shown that food can help calm you and reduce your nervousness. Make sure that hunger is not contributing to your anxiety. A piece of fruit, yogurt, or a sandwich can improve how you are feeling. Because they eventually deplete rather than restore your energy, avoid junk food and high-sugar snacks.

4. **Get enough sleep**
   Your body needs to sleep regularly to rebuild itself and restore your energy. During busy projects, it is easy to work too much and not get enough rest. This condition, known as **sleep debt**, contributes to physical and mental fatigue and reduces your ability to perform. See Figure B-5.

5. **Engage in some physical activity**
   Regular exercise is not only good for your health, but it helps your body react to stress. Even if you do not exercise consistently, some physical activity can reduce the effects of stress. When you start feeling overwhelmed, take a short walk through the building, climb up and down the stairwells, or do stretching exercises at your desk. See Figure B-6.

6. **Use your support network**
   It can be helpful to share your concerns with someone outside of work, especially if you use humor when you do. Spend a few minutes chatting with a trusted friend. Explain your frustrations to your spouse or significant other. Externalizing your stress can help reduce tension.

QUICK TIP
Keep some healthy snacks in your desk.

QUICK TIP
Maintain a regular sleep schedule to help you be at your best and reduce the effects of stress.

QUICK TIP
Be careful not to share sensitive matters with unauthorized people.

YOU TRY IT

1. Use a word processor such as Microsoft Office Word to open the file B-3.doc provided with your Data Files, and save it as Stress.doc in the location where you store your Data Files
2. Read the contents of Stress.doc, which describe an employee's day
3. Offer suggestions to manage stress for this employee
4. Save and close Stress.doc, then submit it to your instructor as requested

FIGURE B-5: Effects of sleep deprivation

Irritability, memory lapses, and lack of focus

Decreased reaction time, aches, and discomfort

Impaired immune system

Increased heart variability

© Jupiterimages Corporation

FIGURE B-6: Physical activity reduces stress

Take a short walk around the building or climb up and down the stairs to refresh yourself

© Jupiterimages Corporation

TABLE B-3: Managing stress do's and don'ts

guideline	do	don't
Remove yourself from stressful situations	• Take a break from a stressful task • Engage in physical activity • Take deep breaths and exhale fully until you feel calm	• **Don't** put off tasks for too long, or you increase the stress they cause • **Don't** ignore physical signs of stress
Use stress to your advantage	Turn the nervous energy that stress causes into productive energy	**Don't** let stress control you
Be aware of your physical responses	• Eat a snack • Get plenty of sleep • Exercise regularly • Take a walk or engage in other physical activity	• **Don't** let hunger contribute to your anxiety • **Don't** snack on high-sugar, low-nutrition junk foods • **Don't** build up a sleep debt by working late and rising early

UNIT
B
Professionalism

Maintaining a Professional Workspace

What you accomplish each day is influenced by your work ethic and your work environment. Whether an office, cubicle, or desk, design and maintain your workspace to support your tasks and reflect the image you want to project. People joke about a messy desk being the sign of a creative mind or genius at work, but studies have found that you can lose several hours of productivity each week when your workspace is messy, unorganized, or not designed to support you. Table B-4 lists the do's and don'ts of maintaining a professional workspace. Tia encourages all Quest employees to keep their desks neat and free of clutter, especially when meeting with customers. You decide to discuss ways to maintain a professional workspace with the new hires.

ESSENTIAL ELEMENTS

1. **Make your space comfortable and inviting**
   You spend a significant amount of time in your workspace—in some cases more time than you spend at home. Invest some time and attention in designing a warm, friendly, and comfortable workspace by setting a photo of your family on your desk or adding other personal items.
2. **Design your space to support your workflow**
   Analyze what you do at work and adjust your workspace accordingly. Put the tools you use the most the closest to you. Remove items that you don't use or are distracting. For example, if you spend a lot of time on the computer, make sure your computer is easy to access but doesn't get in the way of other types of tasks.
3. **Use appropriate lighting**
   Most commercial buildings use overhead fluorescent lights. Although energy efficient, many people find this type of lighting uncomfortable. Some types of fluorescent lights can appear harsh, have a distracting color, or flicker, causing eye strain and headaches. If permitted, an incandescent desk lamp or task light can make your workspace seem warmer and provide extra illumination.
4. **Follow ergonomic principles**
   Ergonomics is the science of designing your workspace to fit you and your body. A properly designed workspace makes you physically comfortable and reduces the chances of repetitive stress injuries. Take time to adjust your seat, desk height, and monitor position. Use accessories such as a lumbar cushion, foot rest, or wrist pad to help match your body to the space. See Figure B-7.
5. **Project the appropriate image**
   The appearance of your workspace tells others a lot about you. Use the same approach to decorating your office that you use when choosing your professional wardrobe. If you work in a conservative department or profession, your office should reflect that standard. Avoid clutter, even in the middle of a busy project. See Figure B-8.

QUICK TIP
Incandescent lights are the screw-in bulbs. Industrial fluorescents are long and tubular.

QUICK TIP
Repetitive stress injuries occur when you do something over and over and your body isn't in the proper position.

QUICK TIP
Be careful not to display anything that is controversial or could be offensive to someone else.

YOU TRY IT

1. **Use a word processor such as Microsoft Office Word to open the file B-4.doc provided with your Data Files, and save it as Workspace.doc in the location where you store your Data Files**
2. **Read the contents of Workspace.doc, which describe an employee's workspace**
3. **Write suggestions for improving the workspace**
4. **Save and close Workspace.doc, then submit it to your instructor as requested**

FIGURE B-7: Ergonomic design

FIGURE B-8: Avoid clutter in your workspace

TABLE B-4: Maintaining a professional workspace do's and don'ts

guideline	do	don't
Design your space	• Make your workspace comfortable and inviting • Include some personal items, if you are allowed to do so • Design your space to support your workflow • Keep the tools you use the most closest to you	• **Don't** make your workspace bare and cold • **Don't** keep items you use infrequently or find distracting near you
Follow ergonomics principles	• Use appropriate lighting • Add softer task lighting • Arrange your desk and chair so you are physically comfortable • Reduce the chance of repetitive stress injuries	• **Don't** suffer from overhead lights that flicker or cast a harsh light • **Don't** work too long in one position
Project a professional image	• Keep your workspace neat and free from clutter • Design your workspace to reflect your department or profession	• **Don't** display items that others might find controversial • **Don't** let clutter accumulate

UNIT B

Professionalism

Taking Advantage of Professional Opportunities

One characteristic of being a professional is that you often have some latitude in your responsibilities and assignments. Be aware that some job assignments do not contribute to your career plans and might actually hurt you professionally. When you have a choice, advance your career by taking advantage of professional opportunities that add to your knowledge, skill set, and visibility in the organization. You ask Tia to discuss her suggestions about taking advantage of professional opportunities at Quest Specialty Travel.

ESSENTIAL ELEMENTS

1. **Keep your career goals in mind**
   Every opportunity that you take advantage of will move you and your career in some direction. Ideally, you want to identify opportunities that can help you reach your professional goals. Project what you would like to do and where you want to be in the short and long term. Consider whether opportunities lead you towards your goal or present obstacles.

> **QUICK TIP**
> You will also have your share of responsibilities that are low profile and do not enjoy the same level of recognition. Be sure to do your best work regardless.

2. **Look for high-visibility opportunities**
   Providing high-quality work is your best bet for advancement, but completing tasks that are visible and important to influential people can pay additional dividends. Assignments, projects, or tasks that contribute to the organization's mission or key sources of revenue are most easily recognized.

3. **Meet key people**
   Volunteer for committees, teams, and task groups that introduce you to and allow you to work with key decision makers in the organization. Developing working relationships with decision makers creates more career opportunities. Expending extra effort and being a good team player in such situations can lead to advancement. See Figure B-9.

> **QUICK TIP**
> Consider training and educational opportunities to be job benefits.

4. **Attend training sessions**
   Businesses provide training sessions to update employee skills and knowledge of their market and products. Take advantage of training opportunities when you can. Do not limit yourself to volunteering for seminars held in attractive locations. Most training is provided in-house or on the job. Cross-training in other areas makes you more versatile, more valuable to your company, and ultimately more marketable when seeking your next employment opportunity. See Figure B-10.

5. **Accept unappealing tasks graciously**
   When you are assigned a task that does not appeal to you, accept the challenge gracefully. Your manager will appreciate your can-do attitude. Taking on lousy assignments can also help you make a case for why you should also be given the good opportunities you are seeking.

YOU TRY IT

1. Use a word processor such as Microsoft Office Word to open the file B-5.doc provided with your Data Files, and save it as Opportunities.doc in the location where you store your Data Files
2. Read the contents of Opportunities.doc, which describe a business encounter
3. Describe how you would react to the opportunities offered
4. Save and close Opportunities.doc, then submit it to your instructor as requested

FIGURE B-9: Strive to meet key people in your organization

© Jupiterimages Corporation

FIGURE B-10: Take advantage of training opportunities

Introduce yourself to others during training sessions

© Jupiterimages Corporation

Professionalism

UNIT
B
Professionalism

Earning Recognition

Many intelligent, hard-working people give their best effort day after day but are rarely recognized for their accomplishments. This is a common source of frustration for many employees and often limits their career advancement. Most managers are too busy to constantly observe and evaluate their employees' work. Successful employees help their bosses understand what they are doing and why it is important. Table B-5 lists the do's and don'ts of earning recognition for your efforts. During your meeting with Tia and the new Quest employees, you offer suggestions for earning recognition for professional efforts.

ESSENTIAL ELEMENTS

1. **Communicate about all of your accomplishments**
   People commonly fail to promote themselves because they believe their responsibilities are routine or mundane. However, activities that are familiar to you might be new or exciting to a senior manager visiting your division. Maintain an optimistic attitude about your job and take advantage of opportunities to share your wins with others.

2. **Give your boss "talking points"**
   Managers are responsible for the productivity of their staff. They frequently have to make presentations or submit reports that highlight the noteworthy accomplishments in their departments. See Figure B-11. Keeping your supervisor briefed on what you are doing and tasks you have completed makes them aware of your work and provides talking points they can use.

QUICK TIP
Having your manager explain to others what you are doing directly benefits your career.

3. **Call attention to yourself by praising others**
   In an organization, the emphasis is on working together and depending on each other to complete tasks and projects. When the team has a success, do not claim the credit for yourself. A better strategy is to generously compliment your teammates and publicly praise the group. The positive acknowledgements create goodwill and reflect favorably on you.

4. **Seek unique tasks**
   People rarely pay attention when you perform routine tasks adequately. Instead, look for responsibilities that are new, different, or exciting. Add unique projects to your task list. When you do the unexpected, people naturally take notice, especially if your performance is outstanding.

5. **Take advantage of promotional opportunities**
   Many organizations—especially larger ones—use a variety of internal communication tools, such as newsletters, internal blogs, bulletin boards, and employee-training seminars. See Figure B-12. Contribute to these resources regularly. Write a newsletter article about your project, or lead a training session for other employees. Top management pays attention and might reward you.

QUICK TIP
Newsletter editors are usually eager for material and will welcome your submission

6. **Network across the organization**
   Although you want to impress your immediate supervisor and colleagues, do not overlook people who work in other parts of the organization. Developing a broad network of professional relationships pays off when you are seeking new employment opportunities or promotions.

YOU TRY IT

1. Use a word processor such as Microsoft Office Word to open the file B-6.doc provided with your Data Files, and save it as Recognition.doc in the location where you store your Data Files
2. Read the contents of Recognition.doc, which describe a business conversation
3. List the pros and cons of the employee's speech habits
4. Save and close Recognition.doc, then submit it to your instructor as requested

FIGURE B-11: Give your boss talking points

© Jupiterimages Corporation

FIGURE B-12: Volunteer to lead a training session

© Jupiterimages Corporation

Professionalism

TABLE B-5: Earning recognition do's and don'ts

guideline	do	don't
Communicate about your accomplishments	• Keep in mind that activities familiar to you might be innovative to others • Share your successes with others • Give your boss talking points	**Don't** fail to promote yourself because you think your responsibilities are routine or mundane
Praise others	• Compliment teammates • Publicly praise group accomplishments	**Don't** claim a team success as your own
Seek promotional opportunities	• Accept or volunteer for unique tasks and projects • Perform new tasks exceptionally well • Contribute to internal communication resources, such as newsletters and blogs • Network with other employees outside your department	• **Don't** accept an unusual responsibility and then fail to perform it well • **Don't** overlook people and opportunities in other parts of the organization

UNIT

B

Professionalism

Technology @ Work: Online Calendar Tools

ESSENTIAL ELEMENTS

The Web offers dozens of calendar tools to help you and your team schedule tasks and meet deadlines. Many of these online calendars let you share a calendar with others to coordinate meetings and other activities. If you keep a calendar on your smartphone, you can synchronize that calendar with the online one to keep your schedules up to date. Figure B-13 shows the calendar synchronization tools for the Apple iPhone (*www.apple.com/mobileme*). Some online calendars are designed to let you host a calendar that others use to find free time slots—an ideal tool if you are scheduling training sessions or conferences. If you want to display a calendar on your Web site that displays events related to your organization, you can publish a calendar such as the Web Calendar Pad (*www.calendarpad.com*). See Figure B-14. At this site, you can also design and then print a calendar to post on a bulletin board. Tia Patterson spends a lot of time coordinating schedules for training sessions. She asks you to review the available online calendar tools so she can identify one that serves her needs.

QUICK TIP

Make sure your e-mail software can react to messages that schedule events or respond to invitations before committing to an online calendar.

1. **Share a calendar**

   The main advantage of online calendars is that you can access your schedule even if you are not working on your computer. Share an online calendar such as Google Calendar (*www.google.com/calendar*) or Yahoo! Calendar (*calendar.yahoo.com*) to coordinate activities with others. Both tools have long-term calendars, let many users share schedules, and send messages to your e-mail program or mobile device.

2. **Synchronize calendars**

   Most online calendars synchronize with devices such as portable digital assistants (PDAs) and smartphones. Other software tools are designed to synchronize calendars you store on various computing devices. For example, NuevaSync (*www.nuevasync.com*), Calgoo (*www.calgoo.com*), and Apple's MobileMe synchronize calendars on your computer and your smartphone. BusyMac (*www.busymac.com*) and Spanning Sync (*www.spanningsync.com*) can synchronize Apple iCal online calendars with Google Calendar.

3. **Send e-mail reminders**

   If you want to remind others about an upcoming or recurring meeting or training session, for example, use an online calendar such as Google Calendar or Yahoo! Calendar to send out reminder e-mails before the event to all participants.

4. **Maintain shift schedules**

   If your organization works in shifts that demand frequently changing schedules, use a shift-staffing calendar such as Shiftboard (*www.shiftboard.com*) or various desktop gadgets available for Windows Vista and Windows 7. These shift calendars are also appropriate for organizations that need to schedule time for volunteers or outside contractors.

YOU TRY IT

1. **Open a Web browser such as Microsoft Internet Explorer or Mozilla Firefox, and visit a Web site mentioned in this lesson**
2. **Using the instructions on the Web site or available through Help, set up a calendar that schedules events for the upcoming month**
3. **Press the Print Screen key to take a screen shot of your calendar, open a word-processing program such as Microsoft Word, press Ctrl+V to paste the screen shot in a new document, and then and send the document to your instructor**

FIGURE B-13: Synchronization tools for the Apple iPhone

apple.com

FIGURE B-14: Web Calendar Pad

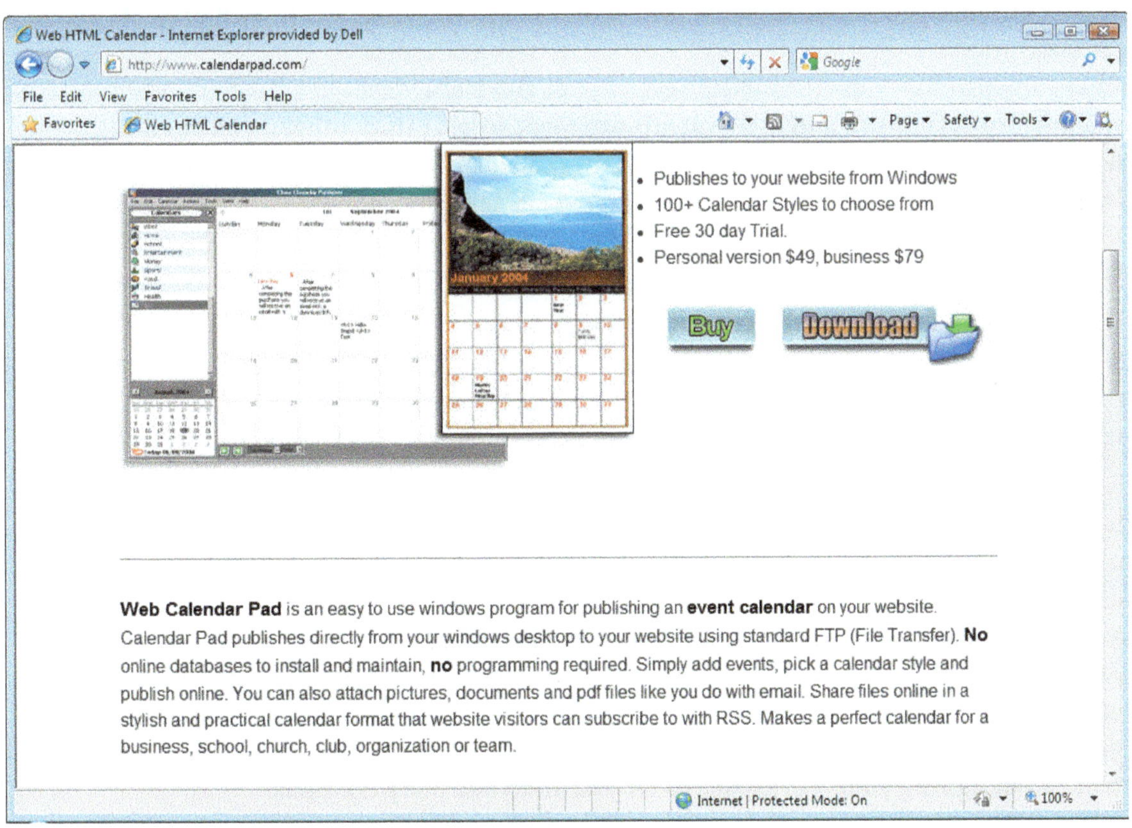

Calendar Pad.com

Practice

▼ SOFT SKILLS REVIEW

Demonstrate your work ethic and commitment.

1. **Which of the following is *not* a way to demonstrate your work ethic?**
   - **a.** Exceed expectations
   - **b.** Assist others
   - **c.** Act as if others are depending on you
   - **d.** Assign a low priority to shared commitments
2. ***Work ethic* is a complex term that includes personal characteristics such as:**
   - **a.** punctuality
   - **b.** effort
   - **c.** dependability
   - **d.** all of the above

Be dependable and reliable.

1. **Someone who can perform a job under routine circumstances and act responsibly when the unexpected occurs is considered:**
   - **a.** variable
   - **b.** reliable
   - **c.** punctual
   - **d.** undependable
2. **How can you practice consistent attendance habits?**
   - **a.** Take a vacation every 2 months
   - **b.** Attend conferences only when it is convenient
   - **c.** Be punctual to scheduled events
   - **d.** All of the above

Manage your time.

1. **Tools and techniques you use to schedule time and accomplish tasks, goals, and projects are called:**
   - **a.** time management
   - **b.** schedulers
   - **c.** task management
   - **d.** goal management
2. **Because some projects, tasks, and assignments are more urgent than others, you should:**
   - **a.** attend meetings before work
   - **b.** vary the types of tasks you perform
   - **c.** wait until you have plenty of time to work on urgent tasks
   - **d.** set priorities

Manage stress.

1. **What should you do when your stress level is rising?**
   - **a.** Work a little harder
   - **b.** Take a break
   - **c.** Hang a "Do Not Disturb" sign on your desk
   - **d.** Lose your temper
2. **What is it called when you consistently work too much and fail to get enough rest?**
   - **a.** Stress debt
   - **b.** Sleep debt
   - **c.** Work ethic overload
   - **d.** Stress overload

Maintain a professional workspace.

1. **Should a professional workspace be comfortable and inviting?**
   - **a.** Yes
   - **b.** No
   - **c.** Only if you work directly with customers
   - **d.** Only if your colleagues' workspace is comfortable and inviting
2. **The science of designing your workspace to fit you and your body is called:**
   - **a.** economics
   - **b.** lumbar design
   - **c.** ergonomics
   - **d.** professional design

Take advantage of professional opportunities.

1. **Which types of assignments, projects, and tasks are considered high-visibility opportunities?**
   - **a.** Those that contribute to the organization's mission
   - **b.** Those that do not contribute to your career plans
   - **c.** Those that no one else wants to perform
   - **d.** Those that involve high stress levels
2. **Which of the following is *not* an advisable way to take advantage of professional opportunities?**
   - **a.** Provide high-quality work when assigned tasks
   - **b.** Meet key people
   - **c.** Avoid unappealing tasks
   - **d.** Attend training sessions

Earn recognition.

1. **If your manager is too busy to observe and evaluate your work, you should:**
   - **a.** describe to your manager what you are doing and why it is important
   - **b.** schedule time for the manager to observe you
   - **c.** start looking for a job in another department
   - **d.** claim all the credit for a team effort
2. **Which of the following is an internal communication tool that can help you earn recognition?**
   - **a.** Personal blog
   - **b.** Company newsletter
   - **c.** Voice mail
   - **d.** Customer meetings

Technology @ work: Online calendar tools.

1. **Why might you want to share a calendar with others?**
   - **a.** To protect your online identity
   - **b.** To submit articles to a company blog
   - **c.** To coordinate meetings
   - **d.** All of the above
2. **If you use a calendar on your smartphone, how can you keep that schedule up to date with an online calendar?**
   - **a.** Synchronize the calendars
   - **b.** Print the online calendar
   - **c.** Send e-mail updates to the online calendar
   - **d.** Commit to using only one calendar

CRITICAL THINKING QUESTIONS

1. **Many people develop a strong work ethic before they start working full-time. If you haven't developed a work ethic by then, do you think it's possible to develop one? If so, how?**
2. **Some people who observe the workforce in the United States say that young workers don't have a strong work ethic. Do you agree or disagree? Explain why.**
3. **Suppose you are working in a part-time job and have no plans or desire to advance to a job with more responsibility and compensation. Should you still demonstrate a strong work ethic? Why or why not?**
4. **Business articles and books often highlight people who gained significant success by working hard, committing to their job, and trading short-term pain for long-term gain. Describe someone you know or have heard about that shares these characteristics.**
5. **Do you think a strong work ethic favors employees or employers?**

▼ INDEPENDENT CHALLENGE 1

You are a part-time salesperson working for Dale and Greg Coffman in their business, Coffman Bakery, in Barrington, Illinois. Your duties are to meet grocery store managers at their stores or in your office and sell Coffman Bakery products. Your supervisors emphasize that being dependable and reliable with customers will increase sales for the bakery and promotions for the sales staff. They have identified a few ways to help the salespeople be dependable and reliable with customers. See Figure B-15.

FIGURE B-15

© Jupiterimages Corporation

Personal digital assistant

© Jupiterimages Corporation

Smartphone

© Jupiterimages Corporation

Time management system

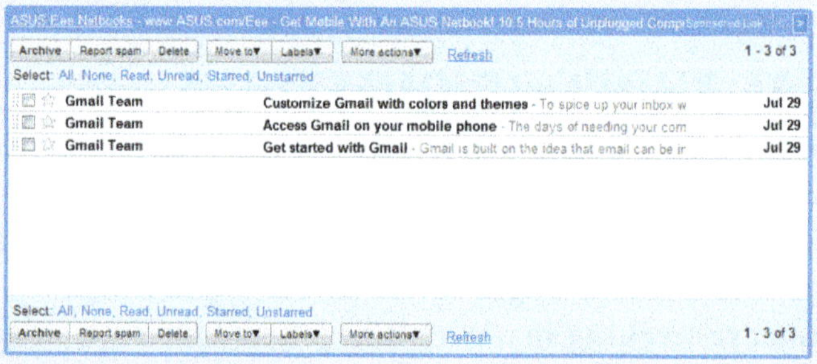

gmail.com

E-mail

a. Use a word processer such as Microsoft Office Word to open the file **B-7.doc** provided with your Data Files, and save it as **Reliable.doc** in the location where you store your Data Files.

b. Select a tool or method illustrated in Figure B-15, and then describe how it can specifically improve your dependability and reliability.

c. Submit the document to your instructor as requested.

▼ INDEPENDENT CHALLENGE 2

You are the front desk manager for Harmony Day Spa in Silver Spring, Maryland. After being featured on a local news program, business at the spa has increased by 35 percent. Louise Harper, the owner of the spa, is delighted to have the new business, but she is also concerned about the additional stress on her employees. She asks you to use the table shown in Figure B-16 to develop guidelines for the staff to follow to manage their stress.

FIGURE B-16

Position	Job description	Guidelines for reducing stress
Front desk	Handle the day-to-day operations of the spa. Greet guests and schedule appointments.	
Sales manager	Generate sales leads, meet with potential customers, demonstrate services, and manage retail sales in the spa.	
Certified therapist	Provide specialized treatments to guests.	
Personal attendant	Guide guests through the spa, escort guests to and from treatment rooms, and maintain cleanliness of spa.	

a. Use a word processer software such as Microsoft Office Word to open the file **B-8.doc** provided with your Data Files, and save it as **Guidelines.doc** in the location where you store your Data Files.
b. Complete the table in Guidelines.doc to list ways to manage stress for each position at the spa.
c. Submit the document to your instructor as requested.

▼ REAL LIFE INDEPENDENT CHALLENGE

You are preparing for a job search and know that employers often seek job candidates with some experience in relevant fields. One way to gain experience in your chosen field is to take advantage of professional opportunities such as training sessions, certifications, internships, volunteer positions, and temporary or contract positions.

a. Using online resources such as career Web sites (*www.monster.com, www.careerbuilder.com,* and *www.jobcentral.com,* for example) and government Web sites such as the Occupational Outlook Handbook (*www.bls.gov/OCO*), research and then list the top five qualifications for a job you desire.

b. Identify two or three ways you can gain experience for this job, such as by attending training sessions, earning certification, participating in an internship, volunteering, or accepting a temporary or contract position. For example, Figure B-17 shows two ways to gain experience in the computer field: by enrolling in an internship and by getting certified.

c. Use local resources such as your local newspaper, colleagues, and job centers to find out how you can participate in the opportunities you identified.

d. Schedule at least one event, and keep track of the details such as your attendance dates, subjects covered, and types of tasks performed. Add the event to your resume.

FIGURE B-17A

ci.brea.ca.us

FIGURE B-17B

CompTIA

▼ TEAM CHALLENGE

You are working for Clean Fields, Inc., a company in Little Rock, Arkansas specializing in recovering land that has been contaminated or polluted. You are part of a project team studying a site near Hot Springs, and will eventually recommend whether the site can be used for building a shopping center. Your manager, Larry Owens, is busy with a different project and has not commented on your team's performance.

a. Work as a team to discuss ways that you can fairly promote your project and the accomplishments of team members without seeming like a show-off.

b. Based on this discussion, individually list four concrete ways to make sure Larry Owens understands your contributions.

c. Working again as a team, make a master list of these concrete suggestions.

d. As a group, select one method that will be the most successful in gaining Larry's attention and demonstrating to him the group's accomplishments.

BE THE CRITIC

You are starting a new job at Meritt Healthcare Products, which provides supplies for hospitals and clinics. You have inherited the workspace of an employee who now works in another department. See Figure B-18. Analyze the workspace, and list what needs to be improved so it is a professional, ergonomic workspace. Send a list of these needed improvements to your instructor.

FIGURE B-18

© Jupiterimages Corporation

UNIT
C
Professionalism

Developing Your Interpersonal Skills

Files You Will Need:

C-1.doc
C-2.doc
C-3.doc
C-4.doc
C-5.doc
C-6.doc
C-7.doc
C-8.doc

How you relate to people you work with can have a bigger impact on your career than how you do your job. The term "interpersonal skills" describes your ability to interact with others. Your interpersonal skills should help you build constructive relationships with colleagues and managers. They should also help you relate to co-workers professionally and socially. People with strong interpersonal skills tend to be more successful in their careers. They get along better with others, influence important decisions, and experience fewer conflicts. In fact, a major part of becoming a professional is developing effective interpersonal skills. Tia Patterson, the director of the Quest Specialty Travel office in New York City, has recently hired many new employees. You have been helping Tia train these employees to become a professional, hard-working staff. Because being successful in the competitive travel industry depends on excellent relationships with customers, vendors, and colleagues, Tia asks you to focus on developing interpersonal skills during the upcoming round of training.

OBJECTIVES

- Understand professional relationships
- Respect social protocols
- Network professionally
- Show basic office courtesies
- Socialize professionally
- Display optimism and enthusiasm
- Recover from difficult interpersonal situations

UNIT C

Professionalism

Understanding Professional Relationships

Many people assume that a college degree, hard work, and good results are the ticket to advancement in their careers. Besides these qualifications, you need to develop appropriate relationships with people you work with. Keep in mind that the decisions to hire you, assign responsibilities to you, and promote you are all made by other people. Working on your interpersonal skills can strengthen your relationships with these decision makers and pave the way to success in your career. Tia Patterson advises you to prepare for the next training session by summarizing how developing professional relationship can benefit employees.

DETAILS

Cultivate strong professional relationships because they:

- **Provide a fulfilling work experience**
  You spend more hours at work over the course of your life than most other activities. Effective interpersonal skills help you develop friendships and working relationships that make your career experiences more satisfying. Work is more enjoyable when you share it with friends and colleagues you know, trust, and respect. Your professional relationships are also more fulfilling when you exchange advice, time, information, and assistance with others. See Figure C-1.

- **Allow you to succeed**
  On your own, you can be responsible only for a limited number of tasks on any project. Your professional relationships allow you to work with others in teams and groups, where you can get more done. As you produce high-quality work and complete projects, you earn rewards from your manager. In this way, working effectively with others mirrors your success in an organization. Most professional jobs involve working with others as a team member. See Figure C-2.

- **Provide the resources you need**
  Knowing or asking the *right* people is usually the best way to accomplish tasks in organizations. They can provide resources such as supplies, equipment, and computer files. To gain access to necessary information, resources, and approvals, you need to know who to approach and how to make a request.

- **Influence decisions**
  Good interpersonal skills and professional relationships can positively influence decisions that affect you. If decision makers know and like you and are familiar with your abilities and accomplishments, performance reviews, task assignments, and promotion decisions will be more favorable for you.

- **Help you find and keep a job**
  A professional network can help you look for and keep a job. Friends, colleagues, and mentors can identify job openings, alert you to advancement opportunities, and act as references. By influencing decision makers, they can also prevent you from losing a job when a company restructures or has layoffs.

FIGURE C-1: Cultivate professional relationships

Work is more fulfilling when you exchange advice, time, information, and assistance

© Jupiterimages Corporation

FIGURE C-2: Professional jobs involve working with others as a team member

© Jupiterimages Corporation

Networking is giving and taking

Some people find employment by responding to a job ad with a resume and well-written cover letter—but most do not. Challenger, Gray & Christmas, an American outplacement firm, recently found that about 80 percent of human resource professionals report networking is the best way to find a job right now. As Phyllis Korkki says in her "Career Couch" column in the *New York Times*, "It's an old saw, but it's true: you are more likely to find your next job through someone you know. The larger that circle of people, and the more you cultivate it, the better off you will be." If asking acquaintances for help feels pushy or intrusive, keep in mind that networking works both ways. Rather than asking others for help, networking should involve a give and take. Anne Baber, cofounder of Contacts Count, a networking training company, explains, "Instead of thinking 'What can I get out of this?' think, 'What can I give to this?'" Korkki expands on this advice. "If you avoid putting people on the spot and are patient and generous," she says, "job opportunities will come about organically, from people who have learned that they can trust you." Dan Schawbel, author of *Me 2.0: Build a Powerful Brand to Achieve Career Success*, suggests innovative networking techniques: "It's the best-connected people who are the most productive at work and have the most helpful mentors. Start today by contacting at least one individual you've never dealt with and asking that person if she or he needs help. The response you get will surprise you."

Sources: Korkki, Phyllis, "You May Not Like It, but Learn to Network," *New York Times*, December 20, 2008; Schawbel, Dan, "Expanding Your Professional Network," *BusinessWeek*, October 13, 2009.

UNIT C

Professionalism

Respecting Social Protocols

Organizations have written policies and unwritten social protocols to guide the actions of employees. A **protocol** is a rule for carrying out an action or behavior. **Social protocols** are the generally understood and accepted ways that govern how people interact with each other. For example, you follow a social protocol when you greet someone by shaking hands. People who do not understand or respect social protocols do not fit into a group. Those who follow the protocols get along more easily with others and command more respect from their colleagues. Table C-1 lists the do's and don'ts of respecting social protocols. During your first training session with Quest employees, you discuss how to respect social protocols.

ESSENTIAL ELEMENTS

QUICK TIP

Even if an organization's protocols seem awkward or inefficient, it is not up to you to change them.

QUICK TIP

Do not bypass your supervisor and discuss concerns or problems with other managers, especially those to whom your supervisor reports.

QUICK TIP

Instead of aligning yourself closely to a group, strive to be someone who gets along well with many people.

1. **Respect how your organization works**

   Every organization has protocols for tasks ranging from arriving at work to requesting new equipment. People often refine and shape these protocols from one year to the next, so they become standard ways of doing business. Instead of criticizing social protocols or explaining how things "should be," learn the protocols and follow them to complete your assignments.

2. **Follow the chain of command**

   The **chain of command** traditionally refers to the line of authority in a military unit through which orders are passed. Businesses also use a chain of command, which you should respect. See Figure C-3. In a chain of command, every employee has a direct supervisor who is responsible for their activities. Employees communicate with their supervisors about their day-to-day work.

3. **Recognize communication channels and power centers**

   Companies typically publish an **organization chart**, which is a diagram showing the structure of the organization. The structure ranks the positions in the company and indicates how they relate to each other. However, these charts do not show informal communication channels or power centers. For example, suppose the organization chart shows that Keisha Lane is in charge of all the Quest branch offices. To get approval for a training topic, you learn that you must talk to Keisha first and then to Nancy MacDonald in Customer Service. In the informal communication channel, both Keisha and Nancy make decisions. Developing friendly relationships with these decision makers improves your chances of obtaining the information and resources you need.

4. **Acknowledge groups and cliques**

   People with common values and identities often band together in an informal group. When a group becomes particularly tight knit, it is known as a **clique**. Groups sometimes develop their own agendas, promote collective goals, and look out for each others' interests.

5. **Consider time and schedules**

   When you need to meet with colleagues, work together, or rely on each other to accomplish tasks, consider schedules, appointments, and deadlines. Make it a habit to be on time, use a scheduling system, and work steadily to meet deadlines. Keep all of your verbal and written communication succinct and efficient.

YOU TRY IT

1. **Use a word processor such as Microsoft Office Word to open the file C-1.doc provided with your Data Files, and save it as Protocols.doc in the location where you store your Data Files**
2. **Read the contents of Protocols.doc, which describe a business situation**
3. **Use the guidelines in this lesson to list how the employee could follow professional protocols more successfully**
4. **Save and close Protocols.doc, then submit it to your instructor as requested**

FIGURE C-3: Typical chain of command in business

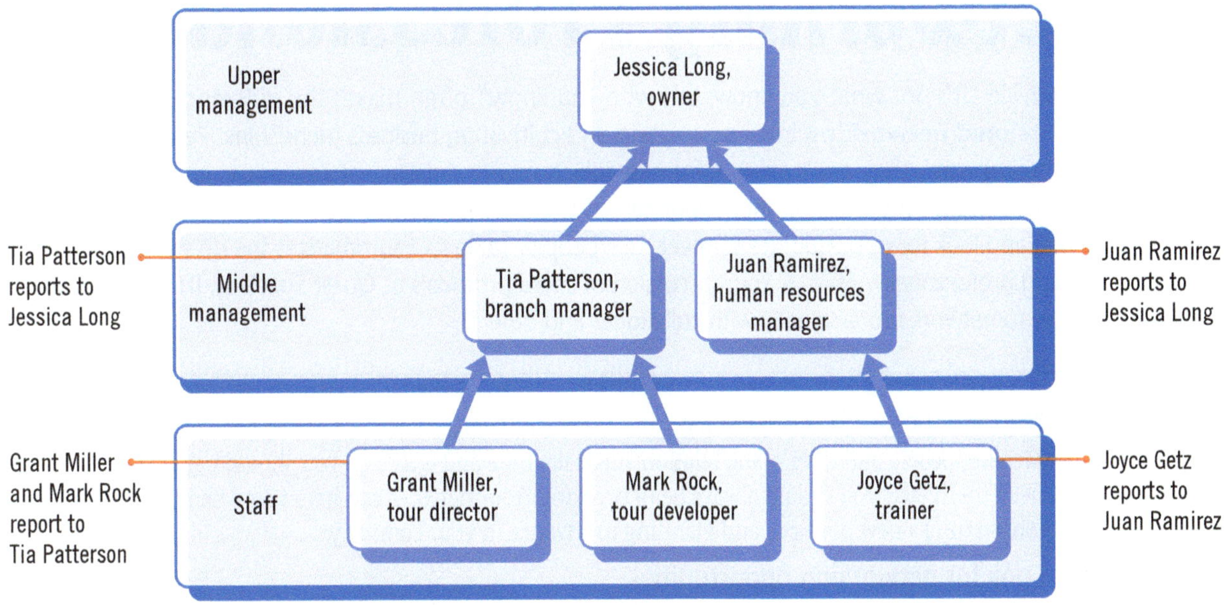

TABLE C-1: Respecting social protocols do's and don'ts

guideline	do	don't
Respect protocols	• Observe how your organization works • Learn protocols and follow them to accomplish tasks • Follow the chain of command	• **Don't** criticize existing social protocols • **Don't** explain how your organization "should" operate • **Don't** bypass your organization's chain of command
Recognize informal groups	• Learn who you should approach to request information or resources • Develop friendly relationships with people who can provide what you need • Acknowledge groups and cliques and respect them for what they are	• **Don't** overlook communication channels and power centers • **Don't** align yourself with a single group or clique
Consider time and schedules	• Be punctual when you meet or work with others • Use a reliable scheduling system • Track deadlines and work steadily to meet them	• **Don't** take up too much time when meeting with colleagues or managers • **Don't** be wordy when you write or speak

Interpreting organization charts

An organization chart shows the relationships among positions in a company. Charts that are arranged as upside-down trees (called hierarchy charts) show the person with the highest rank at the top of the chart. See Figure C-4. Smaller businesses sometimes include only groups of boxes to show teams. In both cases, a vertical line means a direct relationship between a superior and the jobs that report to him or her. A horizontal line shows people at the same level in the organization, such as managers of departments. Sometimes, the size of the box reflects the amount of authority and responsibility for a position.

FIGURE C-4

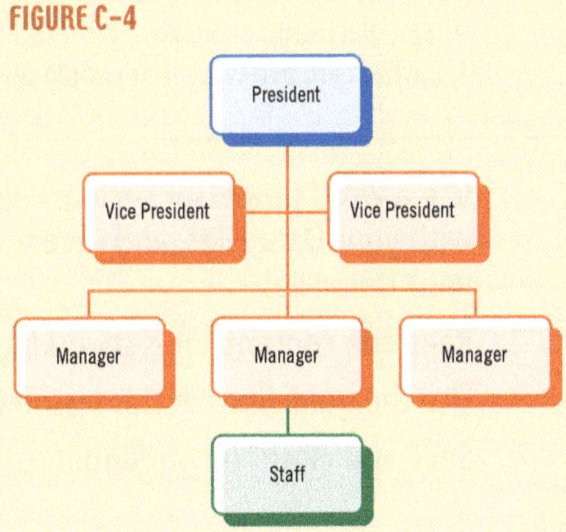

UNIT C
Professionalism

Networking Professionally

The advice "It's not what you know, but who you know" often makes the difference in key decisions. **Professional networking** involves creating and cultivating business friendships. People often think of networking when they are looking for a new job, but your network of colleagues and friends can offer information and support throughout your career. Continually work on developing your relationships with others, and look for opportunities to meet new people. Table C-2 summarizes the do's and don'ts of networking professionally. Your discussion of social protocols at Quest Specialty Travel naturally leads to how to network professionally with colleagues and others.

ESSENTIAL ELEMENTS

1. **Network before it is necessary**
   Meeting people and developing relationships take time and effort, so you should network long before you need to. In fact, you should always be networking. Your network can help you when you are looking for a job, starting a new position, and planning to advance in your company.
2. **Look for networking opportunities**
   If you spend most of your time with the same people, you might miss an opportunity to meet an excellent mentor or professional contact. Seek chances to meet other professionals at business and social gatherings. For example, look for professionals at your organization, in your industry or field, and at professional Web sites, conferences, and training sessions. See Figure C-5.
3. **Distribute and collect business cards**
   Business cards provide information about you and your company. They list contact numbers, such as phone numbers and e-mail addresses. Share your business card with people you meet so they can remember your name and get in touch easily. Organizations typically have business cards printed for managers and other professionals. See Figure C-6. Make a habit of carrying cards with you, exchanging them during introductions, and saving them for later reference.
4. **Prepare to converse**
   Plan what you can talk about when you meet someone you know or are introduced to someone new. Doing so increases your **verbal fluency** and makes you more comfortable when conversing. Be prepared to talk about yourself and ask questions to encourage others to talk about themselves.
5. **Follow up with people you meet**
   Help people remember you by following up after you meet someone. A day or two after being introduced to a new person, refer to his or her business card and send an e-mail message or short note. For example, mention your initial conversation, offer follow-up information, express your pleasure at meeting them, and suggest that you keep in touch.
6. **Stay in touch**
   Strong relationships remain strong if you keep them fresh. Contact people with occasional quick phone calls or electronic messages. Share information such as a relevant article or address to an interesting Web site, which are two ways that people maintain a network.

QUICK TIP
If your firm does not provide business cards, you can make them at a print shop, copy store, or Web site.

QUICK TIP
Look for ways to provide something of value to those in your network.

YOU TRY IT

1. **Use a word processor such as Microsoft Office Word to open the file C-2.doc provided with your Data Files, and save it as Networking.doc in the location where you store your Data Files**
2. **Read the contents of Networking.doc, which describe a business situation**
3. **Use the guidelines in this lesson to describe how to network**
4. **Save and close Networking.doc, then submit it to your instructor as requested**

FIGURE C-5: Take advantage of networking opportunities

© Jupiterimages Corporation

Training session

© Jupiterimages Corporation

Conference

FIGURE C-6: Business card

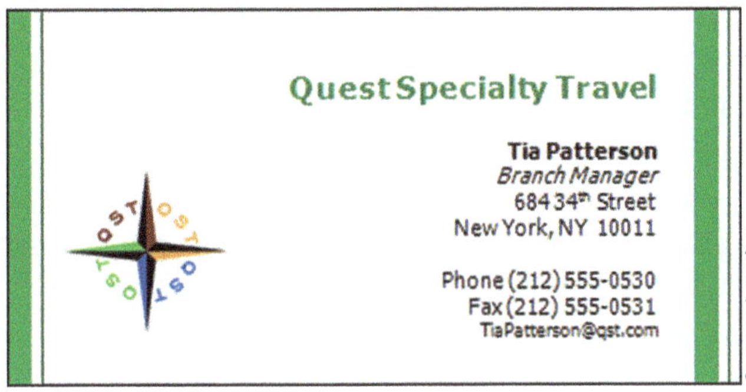

Cengage Learning

TABLE C-2: Networking professionally do's and don'ts

guideline	do	don't
Network whenever possible	• Meet people and develop professional relationships before you need to • Look for networking opportunities • Seek new professionals in business and social situations	• **Don't** stop networking • **Don't** spend most of your time with the same people and in the same places
Use business cards	• Distribute and collect business cards • Share business cards with people you meet	• **Don't** rely on your organization for your business cards—if it doesn't provide business cards, you can print them yourself • **Don't** leave your business cards behind when you are attending a professional gathering
Communicate with the people in your network	• Be prepared to converse when you encounter someone • Plan conversation openers and questions • Follow up with people you meet • Make a brief phone call or send an electronic message • Stay in touch	• **Don't** ignore an opportunity to make brief contact with someone new or a member of your network • **Don't** leave it up to a new acquaintance to make the next contact

UNIT C

Professionalism

Showing Basic Office Courtesies

On the job, you demonstrate your interpersonal skills in how you generally conduct yourself. People observe you and make judgments about your behavior based on your formal interactions with them, how you act in informal settings, and how you treat other people. You can strengthen your image as a polite, professional colleague by consistently following the rules of office etiquette. Table C-3 summarizes the do's and don'ts of showing basic office courtesies. Tia Patterson values courtesy and civility among the Quest staff, so she asks you to devote some training time to basic office courtesies.

ESSENTIAL ELEMENTS

1. **Exchange pleasantries**

   At the office, pleasantries include greeting people when you see them each day and wishing them a good evening when you leave. Use polite expressions such as "please," "thank you," and "excuse me" when appropriate. Make polite requests even if you are giving directions for completing a routine task. See Figure C-7.

2. **Treat everyone with respect**

   Most people are respectful of their managers and other important people in the organization. However, also make a special effort to be polite to administrative professionals, cashiers, janitors, delivery people, security guards, and others that help keep the organization running smoothly.

3. **Offer assistance**

   Offer assistance when you sense that someone needs help. For example, open the door for other people (regardless of gender), hold the elevator, carry packages, and distribute copies. Pitching in with small tasks even if they are not part of your regular job duties generates valuable goodwill.

QUICK TIP

When you can sense that someone needs to hold a private conversation, excuse yourself politely.

4. **Honor others' privacy**

   At most workplaces, many people share common spaces and resources. Respect peoples' need for privacy. Do not eavesdrop on conversations or read the mail, faxes, or computer screen of someone else.

5. **Respect shared areas and resources**

   Follow the backpacker's rule of leaving the trail in better condition than you found it. For example, return borrowed items promptly. Clean up after yourself when using public areas. Restock the copy machine with paper after you use it, and make a fresh pot of coffee if you take the last cup. If equipment needs repairs, call someone who can fix it.

QUICK TIP

It's poor form to push your office mates to buy fundraiser items.

6. **Contribute when asked**

   When asked to contribute to a cause, either for your coworkers or the community at large, contribute what you can. For example, you can contribute to birthday and wedding gifts and to charity collections. Be cheerful and participate when asked. Your donation does not need to be the largest, but you should be consistent in your participation.

YOU TRY IT

1. **Use a word processor such as Microsoft Office Word to open the file C-3.doc provided with your Data Files, and save it as Courtesy.doc in the location where you store your Data Files**
2. **Read the contents of Courtesy.doc, which describe a business situation**
3. **Use the guidelines in this lesson to list how the employee could demonstrate more professional courtesy**
4. **Save and close Courtesy.doc, then submit it to your instructor as requested**

FIGURE C-7: Exchange pleasantries in the workplace

Greet coworkers with a smile when you enter their workspace

TABLE C-3: Showing basic office courtesies do's and don'ts

guideline	do	don't
Be courteous and gracious	• Exchange pleasantries when you greet people and when you leave them • Use standard polite expressions such as "please" and "thank you" • Make requests politely, even if you are giving instructions • Treat everyone with respect • Offer assistance when anyone needs it	• **Don't** give instructions with a demanding tone or language • **Don't** fail to be polite to everyone in your organization • **Don't** neglect others' requests for help when the requests are not part of your job
Respect privacy, space, and resources	• Honor the privacy of your coworkers • Leave shared spaces in good condition • Take the initiative to restock supplies as necessary	• **Don't** eavesdrop on conversations or read others' mail, faxes, or computer screen • **Don't** leave a shared space such as a kitchen or conference room cluttered or messy • **Don't** ignore a tool or piece of equipment that needs maintenance or repair
Contribute when asked	• Consistently contribute to causes, charities, and collective gifts • Respond to requests with good cheer	• **Don't** feel you must contribute more than anyone else • **Don't** contribute to some charities and collections but not others

Manners do matter

Peter Drucker was an influential management consultant and writer who worked with many major corporations around the world. Although he focused on profits and losses as much as any other business consultant, he wrote, "Manners are the lubricating oil of an organization. . .Manners—simple things like saying 'please' and 'thank you' and knowing a person's name or asking after her family—enable two people to work together whether they like each other or not." On the other hand, "Bad manners rub people raw; they do leave permanent scars." Yet observers of contemporary businesses note that courtesy and civility is on the decline in the workplace. A recent study by the New Zealand Institute of Management found that about 90 percent of employees reported at least one episode of mistreatment from a colleague over the last year. That lack of basic courtesy causes problems for the employee and the company. Only 45 percent of people who experienced moderate rudeness were likely to be engaged at work. In contrast, 65 percent of people who did not experience incivility were likely to be engaged. Marshall Goldsmith, author of *What Got You Here Won't Get You There: How Successful People Become Even More Successful*, identifies poor interpersonal habits such as speaking when angry, focusing on the negative, making excuses, claiming undeserved credit, not listening well, and "failing to express gratitude—the most basic form of bad manners."

Source: Wartzman, Rick, "Why Manners Matter at Work," *BusinessWeek*, August 14, 2008.

UNIT C
Professionalism

Socializing Professionally

ESSENTIAL ELEMENTS

Many organizations have a social culture. Employees regularly have lunch together, go out for drinks after work, and throw occasional office parties. You can attend these events to develop relationships with colleagues and managers. You can also use company social gatherings to meet senior executives. However, when you socialize with coworkers, you are still on the job, even if it is after hours and you are off site. Table C-4 lists the do's and don'ts for socializing professionally. Tia has always encouraged the Quest Specialty Travel staff to develop close working relationships, though she asks you to emphasize the protocols for socializing professionally.

1. **Keep your guard up**
   When you enter a relaxed social environment with coworkers, maintain your professional persona. (A persona is the role you play with others.) See Figure C-8. Avoid behavior that is considered inappropriate at the office. Manage your conversations so they remain professional. Be careful not to engage in gossip, but do listen carefully to what is being shared.
2. **Limit the alcohol**
   Business people often socialize over drinks. However, remember that alcohol lowers your inhibitions and impairs your judgment. Drinking too much alcohol can lead you to do or say things that you will later regret. Limit how much you drink at any office function and be conservative.
3. **Avoid uninvited guests**
   Business fraternization is a way for people from the same organization to meet and socialize away from the office. Frequently, office parties are designed for employees only. Do not assume you can bring a spouse, significant other, or friend unless they are specifically invited.
4. **Rule out flirting**
   Office parties and after-work socials offer a chance to know your coworkers better. Remember that your colleagues are not targets for social conquest. Even casual flirting is unprofessional behavior and can easily be misinterpreted, even considered harassment in some cases.
5. **Approach people you do not know**
   At professional social occasions, introduce yourself to people you do not know or have not met. The nature of a social event lends itself to mingling and making self-introductions. Identify key people that you would like to meet, and look for opportunities to approach them, such as when they are serving themselves refreshments, refilling a drink, or standing alone. See Figure C-9.
6. **Welcome new people**
   It's often stressful for new employees to socialize at work events. They don't know many people and are less likely to be sought out by others. Help new employees feel welcome by introducing yourself and starting a conversation. Getting to know new employees is an excellent way to network with the young professionals who may soon be rising stars in the organization.

QUICK TIP
At professional social occasions, the conversation is usually related to work, which can alienate friends you know in other contexts.

QUICK TIP
Don't interrupt people if they are already engaged in a conversation.

YOU TRY IT

1. **Use a word processor such as Microsoft Office Word to open the file C-4.doc provided with your Data Files, and save it as Socialize.doc in the location where you store your Data Files**
2. **Read the contents of Socialize.doc, which describe a business social event**
3. **Use the guidelines in this lesson to identify appropriate and inappropriate behavior**
4. **Save and close Socialize.doc, then submit it to your instructor as requested**

FIGURE C-8: Maintain your professional persona when socializing

Be professional even in social situations

© Jupiterimages Corporation

FIGURE C-9: Meet new coworkers at social events

Introduce yourself to key people at social events such as company picnics

© Jupiterimages Corporation

TABLE C-4: Socializing professionally do's and don'ts

guideline	do	don't
Act professionally	• Maintain your professional persona • Manage your conversations so they remain professional • Avoid or limit the amount of alcohol your drink • Feel free to order a nonalcoholic drink	• **Don't** let your guard down and engage in behavior that would be inappropriate in the office • **Don't** gossip • **Don't** drink more than one alcoholic drink • **Don't** flirt with coworkers
Get to know your coworkers	• Ask questions to learn more about the people you work with • Introduce yourself to people you do not know yet • Welcome employees who are new to the organization	• **Don't** invite guests from outside of work • **Don't** engage in an exclusive conversation • **Don't** ignore coworkers you do not know

UNIT C
Professionalism

Displaying Optimism and Enthusiasm

ESSENTIAL ELEMENTS

Naturally, you need to be technically proficient to be successful in your work. However, your job skills are often not as important as how you behave and interact with others. People generally prefer working with others who are optimistic and enthusiastic about their activities. How your managers and coworkers perceive your personality plays a major role in how they relate to you. It also helps them evaluate your performance and select opportunities and responsibilities for you. Table C-5 summarizes the do's and don'ts for displaying optimism and enthusiasm. For your next training session, Tia encourages you to discuss how to be optimistic and enthusiastic to promote an upbeat, positive workplace.

QUICK TIP
Smiling before presenting an idea or making a comment makes what you say sound more positive.

1. **Smile frequently**
   Smiling is a natural way of communicating pleasure to others. Some people smile openly and naturally, while others are more reserved. Develop the habit of smiling at others when you greet them, pass them in the hallway, and directly interact with them. People assume that you are a happy, optimistic person and will treat you accordingly.
2. **Show appreciation**
   Everyone wants to feel appreciated and valued for what they do. Make positive comments about people and their work. Be generous with your thanks, and praise the efforts of your coworkers, even if their efforts are part of their regular job responsibilities. People appreciate praise and are more likely to give you their best effort when they know that you recognize and value it.
3. **Listen actively**
   Active listening improves communication and shows that you value and respect people and their ideas. When someone stops by your desk or calls you on the phone, stop working on other tasks and give them your full attention.

QUICK TIP
If you regularly give more than expected to a group's effort, they develop respect for and trust in you.

4. **Support team efforts**
   In business, a good team player is usually more valuable than an individual superstar. Support team efforts, and encourage others to work together cooperatively. Recognize that others have different strengths and weaknesses, and appreciate the contributions that everyone makes.

QUICK TIP
Always be tasteful and professional when using humor at the office.

5. **Show a sense of humor**
   Emphasize the positive to reduce tensions at work. Being upbeat and showing a sense of humor can lower personal barriers and foster goodwill. In addition, focus on compliments, not complaints. People who regularly complain about a project, other people, or the organization create an uncomfortable environment for others. Instead, look for the positive, find opportunities to compliment, and tackle your tasks with enthusiasm. See Figure C-10.

YOU TRY IT

1. **Use a word processor such as Microsoft Office Word to open the file C-5.doc provided with your Data Files, and save it as Optimism.doc in the location where you store your Data Files**
2. **Read the contents of Optimism.doc, which describe a business event**
3. **Use the guidelines in this lesson to identify appropriate ways to show optimism and enthusiasm**
4. **Save and close Optimism.doc, then submit it to your instructor as requested**

FIGURE C-10: Show your enthusiasm and smile

© Jupiterimages Corporation

TABLE C-5: Displaying optimism and enthusiasm do's and don'ts

guideline	do	don't
Show your enthusiasm	• Smile frequently • Frequently praise the efforts of your coworkers • Express your appreciation even for routine tasks • Listen to others with your full attention	• **Don't** take your colleagues' work for granted • **Don't** gossip • **Don't** engage in other activities when you are talking to and listening to someone else
Support team efforts	• Express your support of your team's projects • Encourage others to work together cooperatively • Appreciate the contributions of everyone on your team	**Don't** dismiss a colleague's strengths if they are different from yours
Emphasize the positive	• Show your sense of humor • Make appropriate humorous comments • Focus on compliments, not complaints	• **Don't** tell jokes or humorous stories that anyone might object to • **Don't** complain • **Don't** be quick to find fault

Enthusiastic leaders set the style

Some companies are known for the passion of their leaders and employees. For example, Steven Jobs, the former chief executive officer of Apple Computer, was famous for his enthusiastic presentations of new products. People who have attended his presentations claim they work because "He's excited. . .So [are] the others on the Apple team. And that excitement translates on a level unseen," says MG Siegler in a recent TechCrunch article. Siegler contends that "in most successful companies, the enthusiasm about their product is a key to how well that product is doing." Another example of enthusiastic leaders is Dick Costolo of Twitter. When asked why he joined Twitter, he explained, "My first reaction was, you don't get a chance to work on potentially one of the pivotal companies." Significantly, employees report that they love working at Apple and Twitter. Other companies with enthusiastic workers include Facebook, Netflix, and Zappos. Each of those companies is led by someone passionate about the company: Mark Zuckerberg at Facebook, Reed Hastings at Netflix, and Tony Hsieh at Zappos. If you are looking for a job that breeds enthusiasm, learn first about the company's leader.

Source: Siegler, MG, "The Importance of Enthusiasm in Any Product," TechCrunch, *www.techcrunch.com*, accessed November 5, 2009.

UNIT
C
Professionalism

Recovering from Difficult Interpersonal Situations

Everyone makes mistakes at work, especially during stressful times. If the mistake affects a coworker, it can create discomfort and tension. To recover from a mistake, apologize and try to remedy the error. A proper apology can help people feel better about a mistake, save your dignity, and possibly prevent you from losing your job. Table C-6 lists the do's and don'ts for recovering from difficult interpersonal situations. During your final training session on interpersonal skills, you want to concentrate on how to recover from awkward or difficult encounters, such as misunderstandings and social errors.

ESSENTIAL ELEMENTS

1. **Apologize in person**

   Whether you make a mistake via e-mail, in a letter, or at a meeting, apologize face to face if possible. Doing so conveys your sincerity and lets you watch the other person's reaction and adjust your message accordingly. See Figure C-11. If you cannot meet in person, a telephone call is an acceptable alternative, but impersonal media such as e-mail and text messages are not.

2. **Time apologies carefully**

   Usually, it's best to apologize immediately after you recognize your mistake. Doing so can cool emotions before they heat up and boil over. If you have angered someone, you might need to let the other person cool off before approaching the next day. Waiting longer than a day can complicate the problem as a belated apology is often seen as insincere.

3. **Assume responsibility**

   If you make a mistake, do not share the blame with others or suggest it was caused by circumstances alone. Even if other people played a part in the offense, you cannot apologize for them. Assume responsibility for your mistakes. See Figure C-12.

4. **Correct mistakes**

   If you make a social error in an ongoing business relationship, clarify that you will avoid similar mistakes in the future. Make amends by considering the cause of the mistake and explaining what you plan to change or do differently. Correcting mistakes shows that you care about the relationship and makes it easier for the other person to accept your apology.

5. **Be patient**

   If your apology is not immediately accepted, do not retract it or become defensive. In some cases, the other person may respond angrily. Listen quietly and recognize that you have caused them to feel frustrated. Be humble and thank them for listening to you, and leave the option for reconciliation open. People often want to forgive, but it can be a slow process.

QUICK TIP

An apology that includes an excuse does not sound sincere. Take responsibility and let the other person know you are genuinely sorry.

YOU TRY IT

1. **Use a word processor such as Microsoft Office Word to open the file C-6.doc provided with your Data Files, and save it as Difficult.doc in the location where you store your Data Files**
2. **Read the contents of Difficult.doc, which describe an encounter at work**
3. **Use the guidelines in this lesson to identify how the employees can respond to their difficult interactions**
4. **Save and close Difficult.doc, then submit it to your instructor as requested**

FIGURE C-11: Apologize in person

Making apologies for a mistake face to face emphasizes your sincerity

© Jupiterimages Corporation

FIGURE C-12: Assume responsibility for your mistakes

Admit a mistake as soon as possible and then explain how you will avoid similar errors in the future

© Jupiterimages Corporation

TABLE C-6: Recovering from difficult interpersonal situations do's and don'ts

guideline	do	don't
Apologize for mistakes	• Apologize in person unless it is impossible to do so • Be sensitive to how the other person reacts, and adjust your message accordingly • Apologize immediately unless the other person is very angry • Patiently wait for your apology to be accepted • Listen quietly to the response to your apology • Leave open the option for reconciliation	• **Don't** send an apology as an e-mail or text message • **Don't** wait longer than a day to apologize • **Don't** become defensive or retract an apology if it is not accepted immediately
Correct mistakes	• Assume responsibility for your mistakes • Correct your errors • Explain how you will avoid making similar mistakes	• **Don't** blame others or impersonal circumstances for your mistakes • **Don't** apologize without explaining how you will prevent similar mistakes in the future

UNIT
C
Professionalism

Technology @ Work: Enhancing Your Online Persona

Your online persona can be a liability if it reflects an unprofessional attitude or includes photos, language, or details that might embarrass you. On the other hand, a well-managed online persona can reflect positively on your professionalism, education, and technical competence. A recent survey by ExecuNet found that over 70 percent of recruiters said that finding positive online information about a job prospect would enhance the applicant's chances of getting the job. You can use online tools such as search engines, personal Web sites, online profiles, bookmarks, and blogs to enhance your online persona. Tia usually checks the online personas of candidates she interviews for jobs at Quest Specialty Travel. She suggests you and the new Quest employees discuss how to enhance your online personas.

ESSENTIAL ELEMENTS

1. **Research others in your field**

   Search online for well-known leaders in your field. Carefully review your search results to see how these leaders present themselves online, and then apply what you learn to your own online persona.

2. **Purchase your domain name**

   A **domain name** is the label used to identify a site on the Internet, such as *softskills.org* or *whitehouse.gov*. You can register a domain name inexpensively at a site such as Network Solutions (*www.networksolutions.com*). Search the Web for "domain name registrar" and compare prices. Then you can use your domain name in the Web address for your personal Web page or profile.

3. **Create professional profiles**

   Social networking sites such as LinkedIn (*www.linkedin.com*) and Plaxo (*www.plaxo.com*) have become popular with professionals. See Figure C-13. Creating a profile on these sites is free and allows you to highlight specific job skills and talents.

4. **Post social bookmarks**

   Social bookmarking is a way for you to organize and share links to Web sites and other online resources and helps you communicate your personal and professional interests. Examples of bookmarking sites include Digg (*www.digg.com*), Delicious (*www.delicious.com*), and StumbleUpon (*www.stumbleupon.com*). See Figure C-14.

5. **Maintain a blog**

   A **blog** is a special type of Web page where you can post commentary, event descriptions, or other positive, professional material. You can start your own blog on a free service such as WordPress (*www.wordpress.com*) or Google Blogger (*www.blogger.com*). If you cannot commit to regularly writing your own blog content, you can make comments on other peoples' blogs.

6. **Guard your reputation**

   Keep an eye on your personal reputation by using Google Alerts (*www.google.com/alerts*) to monitor the Web for new content that might affect you. For example, create alerts to track your name, your organization, or companies you'd like to work for.

QUICK TIP

If your industry or profession has a special site for professionals in the field, take advantage of it.

QUICK TIP

Share only appropriate bookmarks and links.

QUICK TIP

Blogs are generally easy to create and maintain and do not require Web development skills.

YOU TRY IT

1. **Open a Web browser such as Microsoft Internet Explorer or Mozilla Firefox, and visit a Web site mentioned in this lesson**
2. **Register at one of the sites mentioned in this lesson, and then contribute material about your professional goals**
3. **Press the Print Screen key to take a screen shot of this online content, open a word-processing program such as Microsoft Word, press Ctrl+V to paste the screen shot in a new document, and then send the document to your instructor**

FIGURE C-13: Profiles let you control your online persona

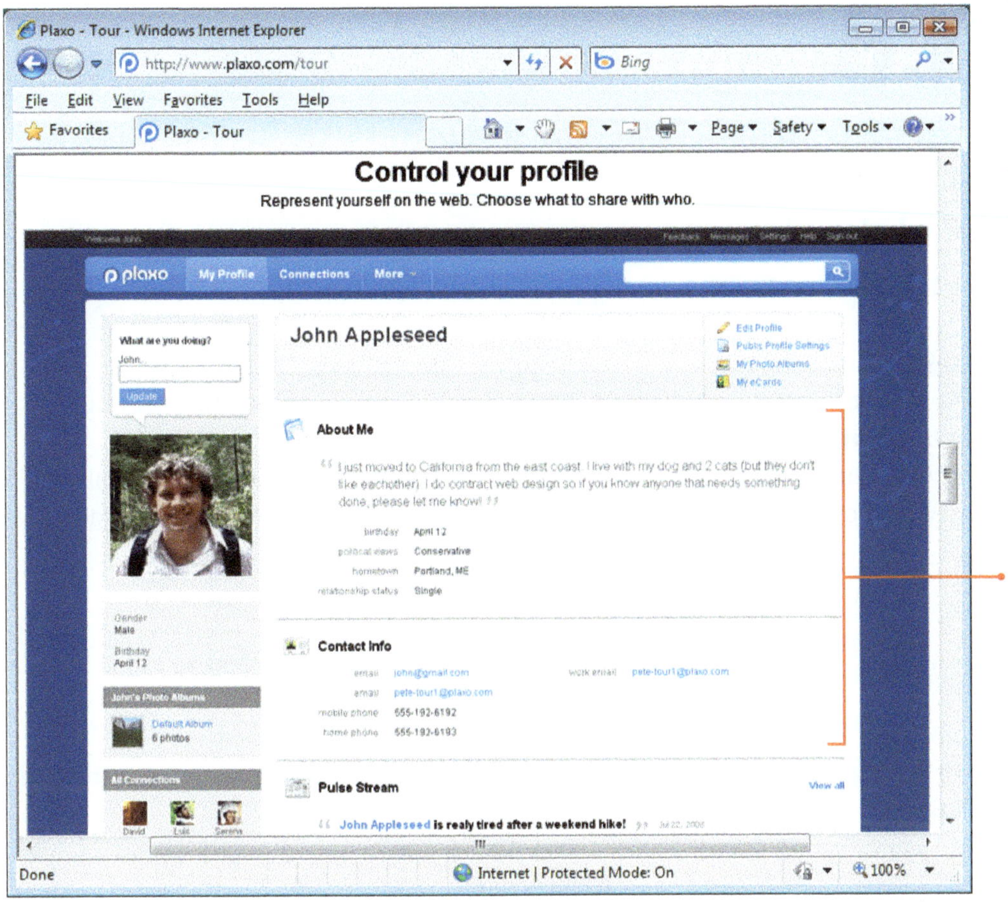

plaxo.com

FIGURE C-14: Social bookmarking sites let you share Web resources

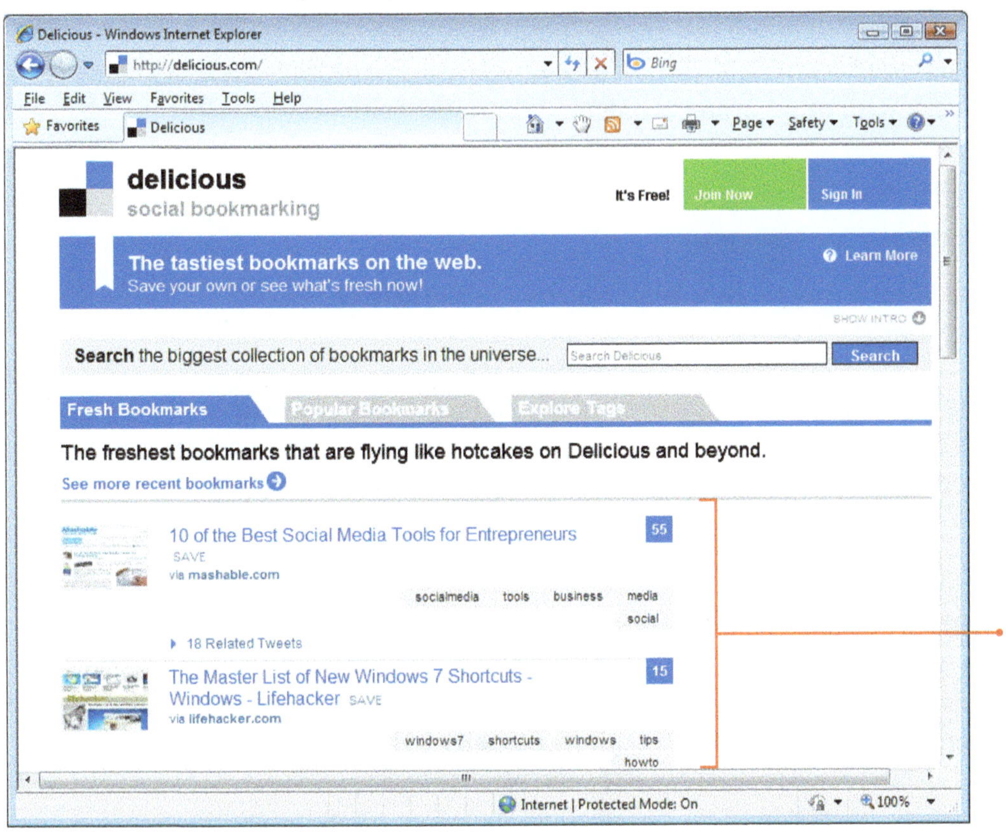

delicious.com

Professionalism

Practice

▼ SOFT SKILLS REVIEW

Understand professional relationships.

1. **Which of the following is *not* a way that developing professional relationships can benefit you and your career?**
   - **a.** Allows you to work successfully in teams
   - **b.** Add technical qualifications to your resume
   - **c.** Helps you find and keep a job
   - **d.** Makes your career experiences more satisfying
2. **Which of the following is an innovative way to network with others?**
   - **a.** Ask a new colleague if he or she needs help
   - **b.** Ask an old friend to review your online persona
   - **c.** Delete everything you find about yourself online
   - **d.** Send text messages to your closest circle of colleagues

Respect social protocols.

1. **What is a protocol?**
   - **a.** A written policy on how to do your job
   - **b.** A common workplace procedure
   - **c.** An unwritten rule that directs how an action or behavior should be performed
   - **d.** A printed instruction guide
2. **When every employee in an organization has a direct supervisor responsible for their activities, the organization is following a(n):**
   - **a.** command chart
   - **b.** chain of command
   - **c.** organization chain
   - **d.** blueprint

Network professionally.

1. **Professional networking is:**
   - **a.** demonstrating business etiquette
   - **b.** following an organization chart
   - **c.** one of many social protocols
   - **d.** creating and cultivating business friendships
2. **When should you network with other professionals?**
   - **a.** When you look for a job
   - **b.** When you start a new position
   - **c.** When you want to advance at your company
   - **d.** All of the above

Show basic office courtesies.

1. **Which of the following is *not* a way to show basic courtesy in the office?**
   - **a.** Keep to yourself and avoid social contact
   - **b.** Exchange pleasantries
   - **c.** Offer assistance
   - **d.** Honor the privacy of coworkers
2. **Which of the following is a way to respect privacy, space, and resources at work?**
   - **a.** Eavesdrop on conversations
   - **b.** Wait to remove your papers from the conference room until next week
   - **c.** Restock common supplies without being asked
   - **d.** Ignore the empty paper tray in the copier

Socialize professionally.

1. **When you socialize with coworkers at a nearby restaurant after work hours, remember that:**
   - **a.** you are still on the job
   - **b.** you are being judged personally, not professionally
   - **c.** unprofessional behavior is acceptable in informal settings
   - **d.** no one will remember if you complain about your boss
2. **Which of the following shows that you are acting professionally with co-workers?**
   - **a.** Gossip about others
   - **b.** Stick to professional topics of conversation
   - **c.** Flirt with coworkers
   - **d.** Drink more than one or two alcoholic drinks

Display optimism and enthusiasm.

1. **Which of the following is *not* a way to demonstrate optimism and enthusiasm?**
   - **a.** Show appreciation for someone's efforts
   - **b.** Listen actively
   - **c.** Make off-color jokes about ethnic groups
   - **d.** Smile frequently
2. **Being upbeat and showing a sense of humor can:**
   - **a.** create rivalries within a team
   - **b.** make up for a lack of technical skills
   - **c.** create an unprofessional image
   - **d.** foster goodwill in the workplace

Recover from difficult interpersonal situations.

1. **When you send an e-mail message to a coworker that creates tension or anger, you should:**
   - **a.** apologize in person
   - **b.** send a formal apology via e-mail
   - **c.** politely ask your coworker to get over it
   - **d.** explain that your office mate actually sent the e-mail
2. **Which of the following is an effective way to apologize for a mistake?**
   - **a.** Immediately send a text message
   - **b.** Wait until next week to approach the person you offended
   - **c.** Explain how you will avoid similar mistakes in the future
   - **d.** Retract the apology if it is not accepted

Technology @ work: Enhance your online persona

1. **Social bookmarking is a way to:**
   - **a.** register your domain name on the Internet
   - **b.** organize and share links to Web sites and other online resources
   - **c.** post comments about professional activities
   - **d.** monitor the Web for new content that affects you
2. **The label used to identify a site on the Internet is called a(n):**
   - **a.** blog
   - **b.** online persona
   - **c.** domain name
   - **d.** Google alert

▼ CRITICAL THINKING QUESTIONS

1. **Career coaches say that professional networking is a valuable job skill. Do you think this extends to networking on the Web at social networking sites? What are the pros and cons of creating and using an online network for career advancement?**
2. **An organization's corporate culture is a combination of its values, processes, and protocols. In short, corporate culture is the way an organization does business. Describe your ideal corporate culture, including the types of interpersonal relationships and professional ethics it encourages.**
3. **This unit makes the point that when you socialize with coworkers, you should behave as if you were still on the job, even if you are meeting outside of the office after hours. Do you think this is fair advice? Why or why not?**
4. **Consider a professional situation where you made a mistake or observed someone making a mistake. How was the mistake handled? Would you now recommend a different approach?**
5. **Prospective employers can legally visit social networking sites such as Facebook and LinkedIn to learn about job candidates. However, when you post material on a social network, do you think your online information should be private, so that you control who can access it and what they can access?**

▼ INDEPENDENT CHALLENGE 1

You are a part-time salesperson at Coffman Bakery and report directly to the owners, Dale and Greg Coffman. In addition to selling Coffman Bakery products, Dale and Greg ask you to help train new employees. They provide the chain of command shown in Figure C-15 to illustrate the supervisors for each employee.

FIGURE C-15

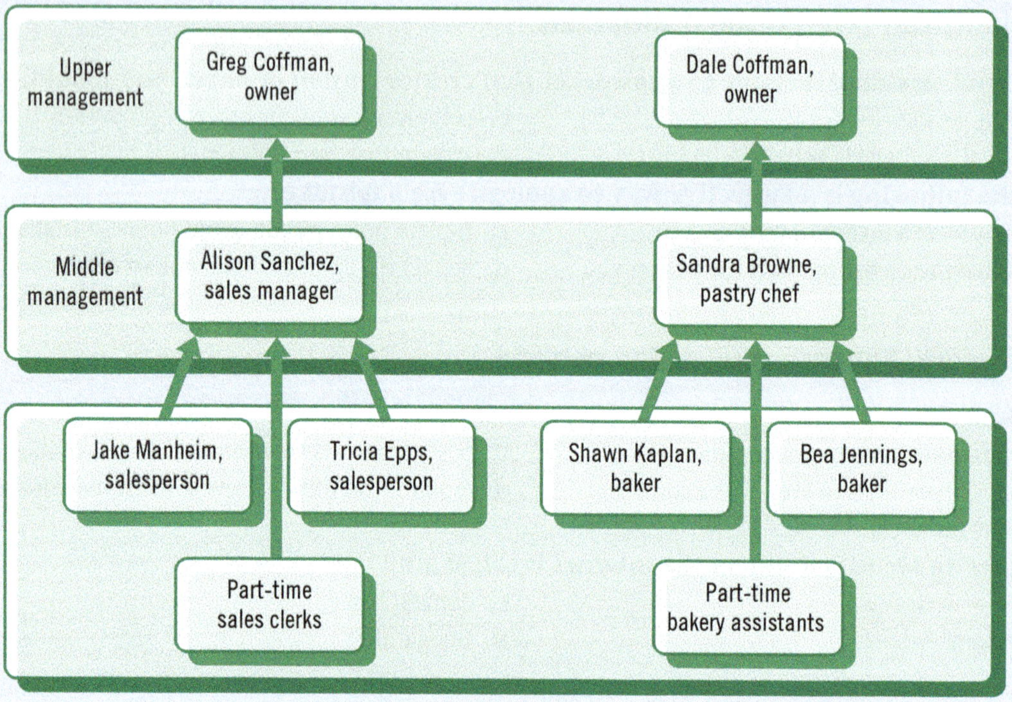

- **a.** Use a word processer such as Microsoft Office Word to open the file **C-7.doc** provided with your Data Files, and save it as **Chain.doc** in the location where you store your Data Files.
- **b.** Read Chain.doc, which describes how two employees resolved problems at Coffman Bakery.
- **c.** Referring to the chain of command illustrated in Figure C-15, describe whether each employee followed the protocols of Coffman Bakery when resolving their problems.
- **d.** Submit the document to your instructor as requested.

▼ INDEPENDENT CHALLENGE 2

As the front desk manager for Harmony Day Spa in Silver Spring, Maryland, you work directly with Louise Harper, the owner of the spa. She invites you to attend a trade show for spa owners and managers. She also encourages you to network at the show because she is confident doing so will help to increase her business. She suggests you prepare for the trade show by identifying specific ways to network when you attend. She has already started a list for you, shown in Figure C-16.

FIGURE C-16

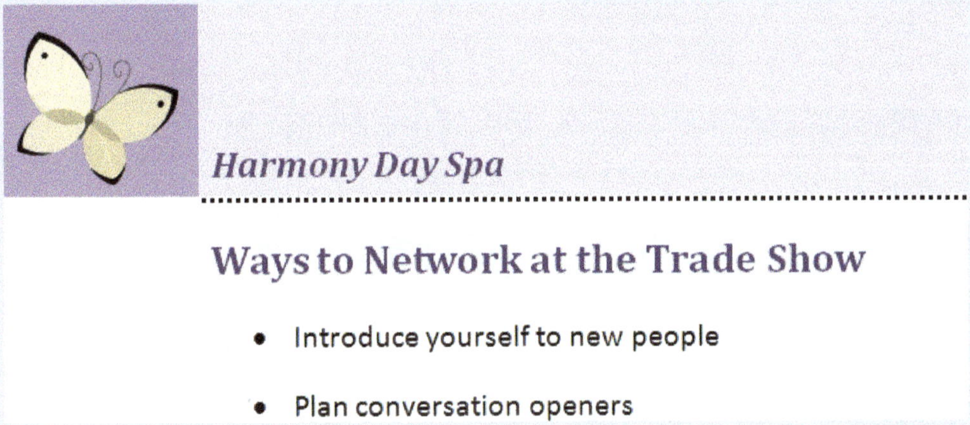
Harmony Day Spa

Ways to Network at the Trade Show

- Introduce yourself to new people
- Plan conversation openers

a. Use a word processer such as Microsoft Office Word to open the file **C-8.doc** provided with your Data Files, and save it as **Trade Show.doc** in the location where you store your Data Files.

b. Complete the list in Trade Show.doc to identify ways to network with the spa owners and managers.

c. Submit the document to your instructor as requested.

REAL LIFE INDEPENDENT CHALLENGE

You are preparing for a job search and know that employers often search online for information about job candidates. You can make sure prospective employers find appropriate information about you by posting a professional profile for yourself.

a. Identify the profession or field in which you are seeking a job.

b. Use online news sources (such as *businessweek.com* or *www.nytimes.com*) or an online encyclopedia to identify a leader in your field or profession. For example, suppose you are interested in computer animation. As Figure C-17 shows, you could look up information about a prominent living animator such as James Baxter in an online encyclopedia, and then search for Web pages where they directly present their online persona.

FIGURE C-17

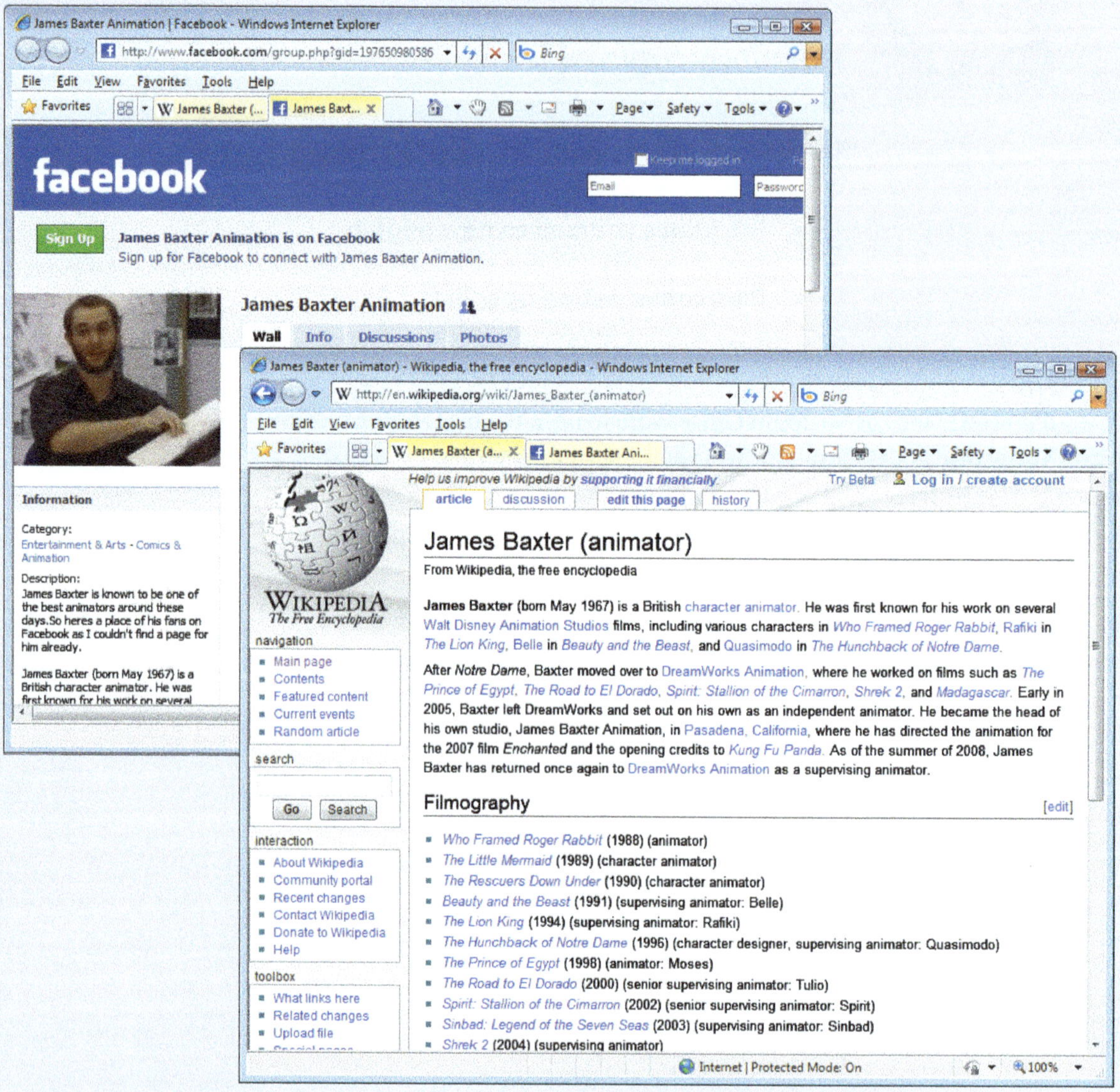

Facebook

Wikipedia

c. Use a search engine such as *google.com* to research your industry leader's online persona. In the search results, look for skills, qualifications, experience, and interests that distinguish him or her.

d. On a social networking site, blog, or personal Web page, modify your personal profile so that it is professional and appropriate for your field.

▼ TEAM CHALLENGE

You are working for Clean Fields, Inc., a company in Little Rock, Arkansas that specializes in recovering polluted land. You are part of a project team studying a site near Hot Springs for a client who wants to build a shopping center. You are meeting with your manager, Larry Owens, to discuss the progress of the project.

a. Work with a partner and select the role of Larry Owens, the manager, or a member of the Hot Springs project team.

b. Larry and the team member meet to discuss the following topics:

- The team has been meeting only every 2 weeks, not every 3 or 4 days.
- Your client has not been returning your phone calls.
- Team members have not been showing basic courtesy to one another.
- You want Larry to meet with the project team.

c. On your own, describe the interactions between the team member and Larry. Also identify how their interactions could be improved.

d. Work again with your partner to compare your descriptions.

e. Compile the descriptions into one master list, and submit it to your instructor.

Professionalism

BE THE CRITIC

You are a new employee at BP Worldwide, a technology company that develops software for businesses. You and other employees in your department are meeting with two BP Worldwide employees from another city. (These two women are seated on the left.) Figure C-18 shows all the employees in a conference room. Analyze the behavior and appearance of the employees and list the positive parts of their interactions. Also list what they could improve in their interactions. Send a list of these strengths and weaknesses to your instructor.

FIGURE C-18

UNIT
D
Professionalism

Winning at Office Politics

Files You Will Need

D-1.doc
D-2.doc
D-3.doc
D-4.doc
D-5.doc
D-6.doc
D-7.doc
D-8.doc
D-9.doc

Office politics is part of every business. Some people consider office politics as dishonest and manipulative. In a more neutral sense, office politics means influencing what happens at work and the way you work with other people. It is a practical part of securing promotions, selling your ideas to others, and gaining the support you need to achieve your goals. People who are successful with office politics earn the respect of others and know how to exchange favors. They also negotiate conflicts and contribute to difficult decisions with tact and ease. Winning at office politics will help advance your career and make your day-to-day work life run more smoothly. Tia Patterson is your supervisor at the Quest Specialty Travel branch in New York City. After hiring many new employees, Tia asked you to hold weekly training sessions on professionalism. This week, you are discussing how to build careers by succeeding at office politics.

OBJECTIVES

- Understand the system
- Identify powerful people
- Cooperate with decision makers
- Develop diplomacy skills
- Choose your battles
- Cultivate allies
- Deal with negative politics
- Develop power and influence

UNIT D
Professionalism

Understanding the System

Every organization has a system for performing tasks, assigning resources, and rewarding accomplishments. Documents such as company handbooks and employee manuals describe parts of the system, such as how to earn vacation time. In contrast, another part of the system is rarely defined in writing. This part is called the **political culture**—the customs, attitudes, and practices that make a company unique. Experienced employees usually understand the political culture so well that they take it for granted. When you start working for a company, you should learn about its political culture through careful observation. Before you start your training session on office politics, Tia encourages you to list questions employees should ask about the political culture when they start a new job.

DETAILS

When starting a new job, answer the following questions:

- **What do the managers pay attention to?**
  Most managers want to meet the company's objectives. Watch your managers closely to learn what grabs their attention. For example, look for repeated discussion topics, meeting agenda items, and memo and e-mail subjects. These help you understand the company's values, goals, and priorities. If you contribute to these goals, managers and other decision makers pay attention to you.

- **Who controls the resources?**
  You use resources to accomplish your assigned tasks. Resources range from basic office supplies to complex computer programs. Someone—usually called the **gatekeeper**—controls access to those resources. Powerful people control many resources. Learn who manages the resources in your company. See Figure D-1. Note their attitude about sharing the resources or making them available to others. You might need to approach gatekeepers diplomatically when requesting a resource.

- **How do employees complete work tasks?**
  Most organizations develop formal and informal ways of completing tasks. For example, a formal rule might require Quest tour planners to meet at least once a week. Informally, this might mean a brief status check after lunch. By following these rules and procedures, employees develop a common understanding of how to work together. Although some practices might seem inefficient or difficult, you should respect the system and work within it.

- **What does the company measure?**
  A common saying in business is, "If you can't measure it, it doesn't exist." Organizations usually measure the activities they value or want to encourage, such as sales, repeat customers, employee attendance, and work quality. Examine your company's forms, reports, and charts. Performance review forms typically list the employee activities a company values. See Figure D-2. Focus your attention on these activities.

- **How does the company reward employees?**
  If you perform well on the job, employers usually reward you with pay raises. Other rewards include commissions, bonuses, promotions, and benefits such as better office space or travel to popular destinations. Ask the human resources department how your company formally evaluates employees. Request a list of the criteria in the evaluation, and then start improving your performance to meet those criteria. Observe who receives rewards outside of normal evaluations and determine why they do. Review your career plan to make sure you are working on skills your company rewards.

FIGURE D-1: Learn who manages the resources

© Jupiterimages Corporation

The gatekeeper controls access to resources in a company

Resources range from office supplies to computer programs

FIGURE D-2: Employee evaluation form

Pay attention to the skills listed on performance review forms

Organizations measure activities they value

Quest Specialty Travel

Employee Performance Review

EMPLOYEE INFORMATION	
Name	Employee ID
Job Title	Date
Department	Manager
Review Period to	

RATINGS					
	1 = Poor	2 = Fair	3 = Satisfactory	4 = Good	5 = Excellent
Job Knowledge	☐	☐	☐	☐	☐
Comments					
Work Quality	☐	☐	☐	☐	☐
Comments					
Attendance/Punctuality	☐	☐	☐	☐	☐
Comments					
Initiative	☐	☐	☐	☐	☐

Quest Specialty Travel

UNIT D

Professionalism

Identifying Powerful People

In an organization, only some people have power, or the ability to influence others to meet goals. Powerful people can help you make progress on your projects or rise to positions of greater responsibility. People gain power through their behavior and relationships, even if they do not hold a title with authority. Powerful people communicate with each other frequently to keep in contact. They also share favors and look out for each other. Often, they influence others outside of their work area, such as in other departments. To be effective with office politics, you need to identify the powerful people in your company and observe how they communicate. Table D-1 outlines the do's and don'ts for identifying powerful people. You begin your training session with new employees by discussing how to identify powerful people.

ESSENTIAL ELEMENTS

1. **Observe interactions**

   When you are a new employee, you do not receive a list of key people to meet to be successful. Instead, you need to observe how others interact. Who acts like the leader in a group? Who makes decisions that others must follow? Through observation, you quickly learn who the leaders are and what they influence.

2. **Follow the promotions**

   As a rule, people who are good at office politics receive promotions more frequently than those who are not. Notice who has ambitions to succeed in the company and whether they advance to higher positions. If they do advance, determine why they are succeeding. You can then strengthen your skills to match theirs.

3. **Find the advisors**

   In every organization, someone provides advice about getting ahead. See Figure D-3. These unofficial advisors often have significant experience in the company and its industry. Based on their advisor role, they have networks of influence throughout the organization. In particular, they often associate with other powerful people. Seek out these advisors and develop a relationship with them.

> **QUICK TIP**
> Advisors can guide you through the maze of the company's systems.

4. **Identify the decision makers**

   Powerful people are decision makers. They might take time to gather information and listen to many points of view, but they eventually take decisive action. When you see others consistently asking someone for resources or approvals, you have found someone with power and influence in the organization.

> **QUICK TIP**
> Meetings are a good place to observe decision makers.

5. **Look behind the curtain**

   Recall that an organization chart shows who is officially responsible for a department or area. The powerful person in that area might be someone else. For example, suppose Keisha Lane is your boss according to the Quest Specialty Travel organization chart. Her assistant, Beverly Cooper, usually approves tour activities and enrollments. For these decisions, Beverly is the powerful person. Be sure you show respect to the person holding the official rank (such as Keisha) as you work directly with the person in power (such as Beverly).

YOU TRY IT

1. **Use a word processor such as Microsoft Office Word to open the file D-1.doc provided with your Data Files, and save it as Power.doc in the location where you store your Data Files**
2. **Read the contents of Power.doc, which describe a business situation**
3. **List how the employee could identify powerful people more successfully**
4. **Save and close Power.doc, then submit it to your instructor as requested**

FIGURE D-3: Find the advisors

Build a relationship with an advisor to learn how your company or field works

Advisors usually have experience in a company and industry

TABLE D-1: Identifying powerful people do's and don'ts

guideline	do	don't
Observe your colleagues and managers	• Observe how your coworkers interact with each other • Identify the leader in a group • Learn what each leader influences in the company • Notice who receives promotions and why they do	• **Don't** expect to receive a list of powerful people you should know • **Don't** resent people who receive promotions—learn from their example
Find advisors and decision makers	• Look for people who give advice about advancing in the company and its industry • Build a relationship with an advisor • Identify people who make decisions • Show respect to people who hold positions of authority	• **Don't** assume you can advance your career on your own • **Don't** rely on the organization chart to identify powerful people

Looking for a mentor

People who work their way from mailroom to the executive suite rarely do so on their own. Instead, they form a relationship with a **mentor**, which is a teacher or trusted counselor. A good mentor can help you learn new talents and practice leadership skills. Ultimately, a mentor encourages you to succeed on your own. How do you find such a valuable person? In an article in *Inc.* magazine, Jamie Walters gives some helpful advice. First, know yourself. "Consider your strengths and weaknesses, and define how a mentor might guide you through your growth," Walters writes. "If you don't know yourself, how can another person support you and help you grow?" Next, find a mentor the same way you find a job—through a network of professional contacts. "Good sources of mentors include your management team, industry associations, online communities, your clergy and/or congregation, and professors." For example, Tom Stemberg, CEO of Staples, chose his business school professor, Walter Salmon, as his mentor. Steve Leveen, cofounder of the Levenger catalog business, found his mentor in a more unconventional way. Leveen read a book called *Minding the Store* by Stanley Marcus, chair emeritus of Neiman Marcus, and then wrote Marcus a fan letter. Marcus became Leveen's mentor when he wrote back. If you are starting a small business and cannot find a mentor i*n your network,* take advantage of organizations such as the Service Corps of Retired Executives Association (*www.score.org*) and the Small Business Development Center (*www.asbdc-us.org*). SCORE offers formal mentoring arrangements, and both offer counseling on business development.

Source: Walters, Jamie, "Seven Tips for Finding *a Great Mentor,*" *Inc. magazine*, April 2, 2001.

UNIT **D**

Professionalism

Cooperating with Decision Makers

ESSENTIAL ELEMENTS

Suppose you think of an amazing idea that would provide great benefit to your company. The right people must learn about your idea and accept your proposal before you can put your concept into practice. That means you must cooperate with the key decision makers in the company. Your goal is to become someone they trust to complete important tasks. You can sell your ideas, secure approvals, and access resources more easily if others see you as a trusted team player. Table D-2 summarizes the do's and don'ts of cooperating with decision makers. Tia Patterson offers to join you when you train new Quest employees on cooperating with decision makers.

1. **Exchange favors**

   To accomplish major career goals, you need the support and respect of key managers, gatekeepers, and political players. Develop these important relationships by exchanging favors. If you help others in their tasks, they will be more inclined to help you reach your goals. Likewise, if you are uncooperative or avoid helping other people, they will treat you the same way.

> **QUICK TIP**
> Always acknowledge the gatekeepers and treat them with respect.

2. **Respect territories**

   Powerful people establish control over other employees, physical space, spending, or a step in the approval process. This area of control is sometimes called their **territory**. If you sidestep their authority in their territory, powerful people can create problems for you. Assume that a gatekeeper controls the resources you need and respect their territory. For example, if Beverly Cooper is the only person who provides final lists of tour participants, don't use a colleague's copy of a preliminary list. Ask Beverly for a final list or wait until she gives one to you.

3. **Offer to share**

   A common favor in business is sharing information or expertise with someone else. This costs you little to give, but can pay back richly later. When you offer favors such as articles, contact information, or instructions, make sure they are valuable to the other person. See Figure D-4.

> **QUICK TIP**
> Say "we" when mentioning accomplishments, as in "During our customer service project, we eliminated 50 percent of common customer complaints."

4. **Promote yourself tactfully**

   Powerful people can promote your career at a company, but they need to know about your talents and skills first. Using discretion, make sure that key people recognize your contributions and capabilities. Look for chances to work on projects or serve on committees with decision makers. See Figure D-5. In discussions, mention your recent accomplishments.

5. **Earn trust**

   Powerful people need others they can depend on. Earn their trust by being impeccably honest with them. Learn to undercommit and overdeliver. Never be late or fail to meet a promised deadline. As you develop trust, you build strong professional relationships with these power players.

YOU TRY IT

1. **Use a word processor such as Microsoft Office Word to open the file D-2.doc provided with your Data Files, and save it as Cooperate.doc in the location where you store your Data Files**
2. **Read the contents of Cooperate.doc, which describe a business situation**
3. **List ways to cooperate with the decision maker in the situation**
4. **Save and close Cooperate.doc, then submit it to your instructor as requested**

FIGURE D-4: Share information with decision makers

Offer articles, contact details, or other information valuable to the other person

FIGURE D-5: Look for opportunities to work with decision makers

In meetings, contribute ideas that key people will find useful

TABLE D-2: Cooperating with decision makers do's and don'ts

guideline	do	don't
Share favors and information	• Help decision makers complete their tasks • Provide information or expertise that others find valuable	**Don't** avoid helping other people
Respect territories and earn trust	• Acknowledge the gatekeepers in your company • Treat powerful people with respect • Be thoroughly honest • Deliver more than you promise	• **Don't** sidestep a decision maker's territory • **Don't** fail to meet a deadline you promised to meet • **Don't** be late in your contacts with decision makers
Promote yourself	• Mention the high-quality work you've done • Promote others on your team along with yourself • Work on projects with key decision makers	• **Don't** take sole credit for a collaborative effort • **Don't** wait until your work is perfect to promote it

UNIT D
Professionalism

Developing Diplomacy Skills

Diplomacy is the art of handling situations without making others defensive or hostile. Everyone in business encounters disputes and other conflicts. When you resolve a conflict with diplomacy, what you say and do helps to diffuse emotions. You reach a resolution that offers benefits to each person in the conflict. They therefore feel better about the resolution. Table D-3 lists the do's and don'ts of developing diplomacy skills. Tia urges you to discuss diplomacy skills in your training session, which should help Quest employees resolve conflicts with clients and others.

ESSENTIAL ELEMENTS

QUICK TIP
Ask questions to make sure that you understand their point of view.

1. **Seek to understand**
   Good diplomacy sometimes involves helping an irate person think rationally. One powerful diplomacy technique is to understand an opposing position before arguing for your point of view. Listen carefully and uncritically to what the other person wants to say. See Figure D-6. Show that you want to understand their objections first. They will be more willing to listen to you in return.

QUICK TIP
Win-win doesn't mean everyone wins equally. Some compromise is still necessary.

2. **Negotiate win-win solutions**
   In the office, conflicts usually occur when people have competing ideas or objectives. Because they are competing, you might assume that one person must win and the other person must lose. However, conflicts do not require a win-lose result. In ideal solutions, each person feels the solution benefits them somehow. To find a win-win solution, ask what the participants in the conflict want and how they can achieve it.

3. **Make people feel good about themselves**
   Complimenting others is a basic diplomacy skill. People naturally want others to recognize and appreciate their efforts. Look for positive comments you can make about your coworkers. For example, thank them for a thoughtful presentation. Mention that their report is appealing and well written. Say you appreciate how they set an example for maintaining a professional appearance.

4. **Agree to disagree**
   At times, even your best diplomatic skills cannot resolve a disagreement. Don't make the mistake of persisting with a conversation that has reached a stalemate. Some win-win solutions acknowledge that two people simply disagree. Agreeing to disagree is a graceful way to end a conflict when you can't reach a solution. It leaves the door open to a positive resolution later. See Figure D-7.

QUICK TIP
A kind e-mail, card, or telephone call make effective olive branches.

5. **Offer olive branches**
   Tense confrontations can be a part of business life. In spite of your best diplomatic efforts, a conversation with a colleague can become emotionally charged and awkward for all. Remember that these confrontations don't last, but the relationships do. Extend an olive branch to your colleague to restore goodwill. For example, say that you appreciate working with them, respect their opinion, and value your relationship.

YOU TRY IT

1. **Use a word processor such as Microsoft Office Word to open the file D-3.doc provided with your Data Files, and save it as Diplomacy.doc in the location where you store your Data Files**
2. **Read the contents of Diplomacy.doc, which describe a business situation**
3. **List the diplomatic skills to use to resolve the situation**
4. **Save and close Diplomacy.doc, then submit it to your instructor as requested**

FIGURE D-6: Diplomacy involves active listening

Listen to make sure you understand an opposing position before explaining your point of view

© Jupiterimages Corporation

FIGURE D-7: Agreeing to disagree can be a graceful way to end a conflict

Acknowledge that you simply disagree—you might find a positive resolution later

© Jupiterimages Corporation

TABLE D-3: Developing diplomacy skills do's and don'ts

guideline	do	don't
Seek to understand	• Understand opposing positions • Listen carefully to the other person • Demonstrate that you want to understand objections	**Don't** interrupt someone when they are explaining their point of view in a conflict
Emphasize the positive	• Look for solutions that benefit everyone in a conflict • Ask participants what they want and how they might achieve it • Compliment others to show that you appreciate their efforts • Make positive comments to help people feel good about themselves	• **Don't** assume one side in a conflict must win and the other must lose • **Don't** settle for a win-lose solution
End a conflict gracefully	• Agree to disagree • Leave the door open to a positive resolution later • Work to preserve the relationship, not the conflict • Restore goodwill	• **Don't** continue a conflict that has reached a stalemate • **Don't** ignore a person after a confrontation with him or her

UNIT
D
Professionalism

Choosing Your Battles

The people in any business hold differing opinions and perspectives. Conflict is a natural extension of these differences. The author Sun Tzu advises that you should "choose your battles wisely." He also writes, "Do not fight battles you cannot win." If you argue frequently with others or oppose most plans, others see you as a confrontational troublemaker. Speak out against important ideas—the ones that stand in the way of your company's goals. Let the smaller matters go. This strategy gives your opinions more weight and credibility. Table D-4 lists the do's and don'ts for choosing your battles. Part of diplomacy is knowing which conflicts are worth the effort. You decide to discuss how to choose your battles as your next training topic.

ESSENTIAL ELEMENTS

QUICK TIP
Make sure the argument can solve a problem.

1. **Decide whether the conflict is worth the fight**

   Win or lose, confrontations cost you something. Participants might suffer bruised egos or harbor resentment. After that, sometimes no clear winner emerges. Before charging into a conflict, ask yourself if the potential payoff is worth the cost. If it is, then proceed diplomatically. Work to reduce the drawbacks. If the costs are too high, consider other courses of action or decide to live with the situation as it is. Figure D-8 outlines how to choose your battles.

QUICK TIP
If you use this strategy, encourage a compromise or resolution soon after you forfeit a minor point.

2. **Sacrifice a battle to win the war**

   You cannot win every battle you have during your professional life. It usually makes sense to sacrifice a small issue to support an important plan or goal. Let others win minor conflicts. When you do, let them know you have given into their requests. Conceding minor disagreements often makes it easier to work toward a compromise acceptable to both of you.

3. **Expect setbacks**

   Reaching your goals rarely proceeds according to plan. Other colleagues get promotions, better offices, or desirable projects before you do. This is a part of professional life. Do not complain about setbacks to your manager or others at work. Instead, work hard to make yourself noticed. Look for new opportunities to demonstrate your skills and abilities.

QUICK TIP
If you decide to say no to a request, do so diplomatically. Suggest someone else who could help, for example.

4. **Select commitments that lead to your goals**

   When the potential payoff is part of your career goals, it makes sense to say yes to requests or stay late and work extra hard on a project. However, watch out for the line between such calculated efforts and being your manager's doormat. Unless you are working towards a specific goal such as a promotion, do not agree to unmanageable projects, deadlines, or obligations.

5. **Focus on the battles you must win**

   To gain a project, goal, or assignment, you probably need to win certain battles. Often these involve persuading a key decision maker, securing an approval, or collecting a needed resource. For example, you might be designing a new tour for Quest Specialty Travel, but Derek Opazo, an important tour developer, might be skeptical about it. Before talking to Derek, do everything you can to prepare for the meeting. Anticipate every question and objection. Ask people in your network to offer advice.

YOU TRY IT

1. **Use a word processor such as Microsoft Office Word to open the file D-4.doc provided with your Data Files, and save it as Battle.doc in the location where you store your Data Files**
2. **Read the contents of Battle.doc, which describe business scenarios**
3. **Explain how you would respond to each scenario**
4. **Save and close Battle.doc, then submit it to your instructor as requested**

FIGURE D-8: Choosing your battles

	High payoff (Leads to career goal)	Low payoff (Not related to career goal)
Few drawbacks (Low cost)	Worth the battle	Sacrifice the battle
Many drawbacks (High cost)	Proceed with caution	Not worth fighting for

TABLE D-4: Choosing your battles do's and don'ts

guideline	do	don't
Evaluate the conflict	• Consider what you gain and lose in the conflict • Work to reduce the drawbacks • Let others win minor conflicts	• **Don't** enter a conflict with high costs and a result that does not lead to a career goal • **Don't** give up on reaching your goals; wait to work towards compromise later
Expect setbacks	• Realize that everyone has setbacks • After a setback, work to be noticed for your accomplishments • Look for new opportunities to demonstrate your skills	• **Don't** think of setbacks as defeats • **Don't** complain about setbacks to your manager or coworkers
Focus on your goals	• Select commitments that lead to your goals • Prepare for battles you must win • Anticipate questions and objections • Restore goodwill	• **Don't** agree to unreasonable requests unless you receive a reward related to your goals • **Don't** enter a must-win confrontation unprepared

On-the-job conflicts

Workplace conflict is inevitable, whether you are an entry-level assistant, independent truck driver, or long-term civil worker. According to Kathryn Schear, a former Equal Employment Opportunity Commission (EEOC) mediator, most people ignore conflicts on the job for as long as they can. However, conflicts that you allow to simmer frequently boil over and create more disruption and stress than the original problem. Schear says warning signs include negativity that lasts more than a week, problems that affect other people in the office, or symptoms of depression or physical stress. At that point, the only solutions are to confront the conflict directly and work things out, or avoid the problem entirely by removing yourself, such as by taking another job. To avoid both drastic alternatives, address the conflict early. Doing so frequently defuses it. Schear recognizes that it is difficult and "scary" to sit down with someone else and talk through a problem. She recommends that you prepare for such a meeting by planning what you are going to say and, most importantly, how you are going to say it.

Source: Dobson, Amy, "Clashing Coworkers," The *San Francisco Chronicle, SFGate.com*, September 14, 2008.

UNIT
D
Professionalism

Cultivating Allies

Even if you are very talented, you need the help of others to achieve career success. Throughout your career, you need the help of those who can support your ideas, offer advice, and look out for you and your interests. Every professional needs to cultivate a network of allies, mentors, and guardian angels to help them in their career. Table D-5 summarizes the do's and don'ts of cultivating allies. Tia suggests that during your training session, you should talk about cultivating allies, mentors, and guardian angels.

ESSENTIAL ELEMENTS

1. **Seek mentors**

   Mentors are successful professionals in your field or company who are willing to meet with you to share their knowledge. People who have been successful in their careers are often happy to guide young professionals. See Figure D-9. You can approach prospective mentors in person and ask them to provide guidance and advice to you. A different type of mentor is a leader in your field who provides an example of how to succeed.

QUICK TIP

A powerful guardian angel can keep your name off the list of layoffs. A less active guardian angel might only warn you about upcoming layoffs.

2. **Use a guardian angel**

   In your professional career, a guardian angel is someone in a position who can look out for you and your career interests. Guardian angels can even meet with decision makers on your behalf. Upper-level managers, administrative assistants, and other well-connected people can serve as your guardian angel. For example, if you have a good relationship with Beverly Cooper at Quest Specialty Travel, she could look out for your interests with Keisha Lane.

3. **Create relationships with peers and support staff**

   Many people in a company can offer you help and support. These people are your allies. Some are often your own peers and members of the administrative staff. Do not overlook those you work with—build relationships with many types of coworkers. See Figure D-10. They can often find information you need, provide access to important resources, or influence others for your benefit.

QUICK TIP

Make sure you are not interrupting anyone when you stop for a visit.

4. **Invest in your relationships**

   Cultivating friends and allies requires time, energy, and money. Plan to invest a certain amount each month for occasional lunches or after-work social events. Use these occasions to build and reinforce your relationship with colleagues. Take time each week for impromptu office visits, hallway chats, and coffee break discussions.

5. **Keep a professional attitude**

   Being an employee is your first responsibility, so make sure your relationships remain professional. Others will feel more comfortable if you are businesslike when you interact with them. For example, signing a card for your manager's birthday is appropriate. Taking him out for an intimate dinner is not.

YOU TRY IT

1. **Use a word processor such as Microsoft Office Word to open the file D-5.doc provided with your Data Files, and save it as Allies.doc in the location where you store your Data Files**
2. **Read the contents of Allies.doc, which describe people in a company**
3. **Identify possible allies, mentors, and guardian angels**
4. **Save and close Allies.doc, then submit it to your instructor as requested**

FIGURE D-9: Mentors can help guide your career

FIGURE D-10: Peers and support staff can be allies

Professionalism

TABLE D-5: Cultivating allies do's and don'ts

guideline	do	don't
Seek allies	• Approach successful people in your company and ask for advice • Look for people who have been successful in your field and follow their example • Build relationships with people who can access key decision makers	**Don't** overlook peers and support staff
Work on the relationships	• Invest time, energy, and money in your professional relationships • Schedule time and budget money for social occasions • Maintain a professional attitude	• **Don't** interrupt others or contact them so often that you become a nuisance • **Don't** let the relationship become more personal than professional

UNIT D
Professionalism

Dealing with Negative Politics

Positive office politics involves building relationships with people at work so you can meet your career goals. In this case, your communication is friendly, cordial, and cooperative. While positive office politics aims to improve a career, negative office politics aims to weaken one. Negative office politics involves destructive gossip, hostility, withheld information, and stolen credit. See Figure D-11. Negative office politics can damage careers and make everyone a loser. Table D-6 outlines the do's and don'ts for dealing with negative politics. After discussing positive office politics, you want to identify ways to deal with negative office politics.

ESSENTIAL ELEMENTS

1. **Focus on company objectives**
   If your confrontation with a coworker becomes hostile, the natural tendency is to find fault with your coworker's positions and opinions. However, that makes it more difficult to resolve the matter with good humor. Instead, focus on the company's objectives rather than your own. Raise questions such as, "What would be in the best interest of our customers?" Arguing about what is best for the organization makes the discussion less personal.

2. **Don't get personal**
   If you become angry with a coworker, it can be tempting to unload and say what you really think. Instead, hold your tongue and cool off first. If necessary, leave the scene diplomatically. People remember insults and humiliations for a long time. Uncontrolled emotions and behavior harm your image, even if the other person provoked you. Rumors and gossip are especially destructive.

   QUICK TIP
   When the conflict is resolved, you will be seen as a peacemaker that everyone can trust.

3. **Avoid taking sides in a battle**
   Finding yourself in the middle of two powerful but opposing professionals is uncomfortable. They might enlist your support to help strengthen their positions. They might encourage you to align yourself with one person or another. However, do not take sides in their battle. Remain objective and help resolve the conflict in a businesslike manner. See Figure D-12.

4. **Widen the audience**
   A conflict can turn negative and personal when only two people are participating. It is more difficult to act unprofessionally in front of an audience of peers. If you sense an argument is becoming personal, unethical, or negative, suggest that other key people join the discussion. Recommend that you take a break and meet again when everyone can be involved.

   QUICK TIP
   Often, suggesting you widen the audience is enough to change the tone of a negative conversation.

5. **Look for a change**
   In some places, negative politics are more the rule than the exception. Changing such a culture is difficult and not appropriate for a new employee. Instead, discreetly visit your human resources office and ask about other internal openings. If the problem is with a team or office mate, ask your supervisor to assign you to a different team.

   QUICK TIP
   If you slip, be sure to apologize quickly.

YOU TRY IT

1. **Use a word processor such as Microsoft Office Word to open the file D-6.doc provided with your Data Files, and save it as Negative.doc in the location where you store your Data Files**
2. **Read the contents of Negative.doc, which describe a business scenario**
3. **Describe how you could react to the negative office politics in the business**
4. **Save and close Negative.doc, then submit it to your instructor as requested**

FIGURE D-11: Rumors and negative gossip are destructive

Gossiping about a colleague can damage your reputation

© Jupiterimages Corporation

FIGURE D-12: Avoid taking sides in a battle

When caught between opposing coworkers, summarize each point of view or say something diplomatic, such as "Both ideas have strengths and would benefit our customers."

© Jupiterimages Corporation

TABLE D-6: Dealing with negative politics do's and don'ts

guideline	do	don't
Remain objective	• Focus on company goals • Raise questions about impersonal interests, such as customer concerns or the company mission • Strive to make the discussion less personal • Keep your emotions in check if you are getting angry • Leave the scene, if necessary	• **Don't** find fault with a coworker's positions and opinions during a negative conversation • **Don't** get personal • **Don't** forget that uncontrolled emotions and behavior harm your image
Avoid taking sides	• Communicate open and fairly • Help resolve the conflict	• **Don't** get caught in the middle of two battling decision makers • **Don't** align yourself with one powerful person against another
Change the environment	• Widen the audience to include other peers and decision makers • Suggest key people join the discussion • Take a break • Request a transfer or reassignment	• **Don't** let a conversation remain personal, unethical, or negative • **Don't** remain in a place where negative office politics are the norm

Professionalism

UNIT
D
Professionalism

Developing Power and Influence

Handling office politics to reach your career goals is essential to your professional success. After understanding office politics and improving skills to build relationships, you can develop your own power and influence. If you are an entry-level employee, you can focus on influencing your immediate coworkers. As you work toward positions of greater responsibility, you can create a power base and communication network with support staff, peers, and key managers. Table D-7 lists the do's and don'ts for developing power and influence. You decide to end your training session on office politics by brainstorming ways to develop power and influence.

ESSENTIAL ELEMENTS

1. **Develop your professional reputation first**
   To cultivate power and influence, people in your company and field should respect you and your work. Set high standards for your work, and then meet them. Be punctual, professional, and dress the way powerful people in your organization do. As you earn the respect of coworkers, you can build on those relationships to create a power base. See Figure D-13.

2. **Respect the system**
   Remember that you are expanding your influence within your organization's system. Be polite and respect the way your company does business. Do not criticize the system or the other players. Learn the system in detail and use it to your advantage.

QUICK TIP

Power is current for a limited time, so you should use it before it expires.

3. **View power as an asset**
   You can think of power and influence as a type of invisible currency. You accumulate it when you do favors for others or gain control over company resources. Make deposits to your power account to keep it fresh. For example, you could do a favor for Derek Opazo by preparing and giving a presentation that he does not have time to give. When you use power to influence a decision or event, you are spending your political capital. In this case, you might ask Derek to assign you to a high-profile tour.

4. **Use your power sparingly**
   You can gather only a limited amount of power, so use it infrequently. People who win at office politics use their power only when necessary. Using it too often might be controlling or dictatorial. In most cases, polite persuasion and subtle influence is more effective. Save the power tactics for when the stakes are high.

5. **Work with powerful people**
   When you work for powerful people, you gain some of their influence for yourself. Take advantage of this by looking for chances to work with key people. Volunteer for important projects or seek out high-profile positions in the company. Remember that high visibility demands excellent performance. Only use this strategy if you can commit to give your best effort.

YOU TRY IT

1. Use a word processor such as Microsoft Office Word to open the file D-7.doc provided with your Data Files, and save it as Influence.doc in the location where you store your Data Files
2. Read the contents of Influence.doc, which describe a business scenario
3. Describe how you could build power and influence in this scenario
4. Save and close Influence.doc, then submit it to your instructor as requested

FIGURE D-13: Earn the respect of your coworkers first

Earn the respect of your colleagues through high-quality work and professionalism

© Jupiterimages Corporation

TABLE D-7: Developing power and influence do's and don'ts

guideline	do	don't
Respect your position	• Develop your professional reputation first • Set high standards for your work and behavior • Earn the respect of your coworkers • Respect the system in your organization	**Don't** criticize the system or your company
Handle power thoughtfully	• View power as an asset • Accumulate power by doing favors for others and working with key people • Spend power on influencing decisions infrequently • Use power and influence only when necessary • Use polite persuasion and subtle influence more often	• **Don't** squander power and influence • **Don't** use power tactics when the stakes are low

Professionalism

Fortune's 25 most powerful people in business

Fortune magazine occasionally publishes lists of the most powerful men and women in business. Any working person can learn from the habits and accomplishments of these business people. Number one on its most recent list is Steve Jobs, the Chairman and CEO of Apple. Jobs doesn't rest on his achievements. As Brent Schlender notes in Fortune, "Jobs has upended [five industries]—computers, Hollywood, music, retailing, and wireless phones. At this moment, no one has more influence over a broader swath of business than Jobs." Bill Gates is number seven on the list. The founder of Microsoft has broadened his power base through the charitable activities of the Bill & Melinda Gates Foundation. Schlender writes, "The foundation has global aspirations to improve health care and reduce poverty. His other goal: reinventing philanthropy itself, much as he did information technology." A. G. Lafley is number ten on the list. Lafley is the Chairman and CEO of Procter & Gamble. Patricia Sellers notes, "By demanding innovation in everything that P&G does," Lafley has steered fading brands such as Tide, Crest, and Gillette to impressive profits.

Source: Schlender, Brent, and Sellers, Patricia, "25 Most Powerful People in Business," Fortune, January 29, 2008.

Technology @ Work: Content Aggregators

Knowledge is power, and the Web is full of information you can turn into knowledge. The well-known problem with the Web is that it provides access to too much information. To make sense of it all, you can use a content aggregator. A **content aggregator** is a Web site that collects certain types of information on the Web. For example, some content aggregators collect articles about entertainment, sports, or politics, and present it in a single online location. Other content aggregators gather syndicated Web content such as news headlines, blogs, podcasts, and video logs (vlogs). You can use an aggregator to reduce your time and effort when you check Web sites for updates. Popurls (*www.popurls.com*, pronounced "populars") is a popular content aggregator that pulls together current headlines from major news and opinion sites, blogs, and vlogs. Tia wants everyone at the Quest New York office to stay on top of travel news. She asks you to find a content aggregator that can provide this type of information.

ESSENTIAL ELEMENTS

1. **Visit the Popurls home page**
   Start by opening the home page of the popurls Web site at *www.popurls.com*. See Figure D-14. The site collects links to the most visited pages on Web sites such as Digg, Delicious, and Twitter, and lists the most popular headlines at those sites.
2. **Scan the links, and then select one**
   Scan the links from other news sites, and then click one that interests you.
3. **Customize the home page**
   You can customize the Popurls home page to suit your interests by clicking the Customize button. Select options to show or hide links from particular Web sites or switch to a view that lists links according to topic or date.
4. **Visit the Popurls blue edition**
   On the Popurls home page, you can click the Popurls blue link to open a different edition of Popurls designed for businesses. See Figure D-15. Like the standard edition, the Popurls blue edition provides quick access to current business news.

YOU TRY IT

1. **Open a Web browser such as Microsoft Internet Explorer or Mozilla Firefox, and visit www.popurls.com**
2. **Find a link related to career advice, office politics, or another topic discussed in this unit, and then click that link**
3. **Take a screen shot of the Web page, and send it to your instructor**
4. **Return to the Popurls home page, and then click the popurls blue link**
5. **Click a link listed in the Popular Today section**
6. **Press the Print Screen key to take a screen shot of the Web page, open a word-processing program such as Microsoft Word, press Ctrl+V to paste the screen shot in a new document, and then send the document to your instructor**

FIGURE D-14: Popurls home page

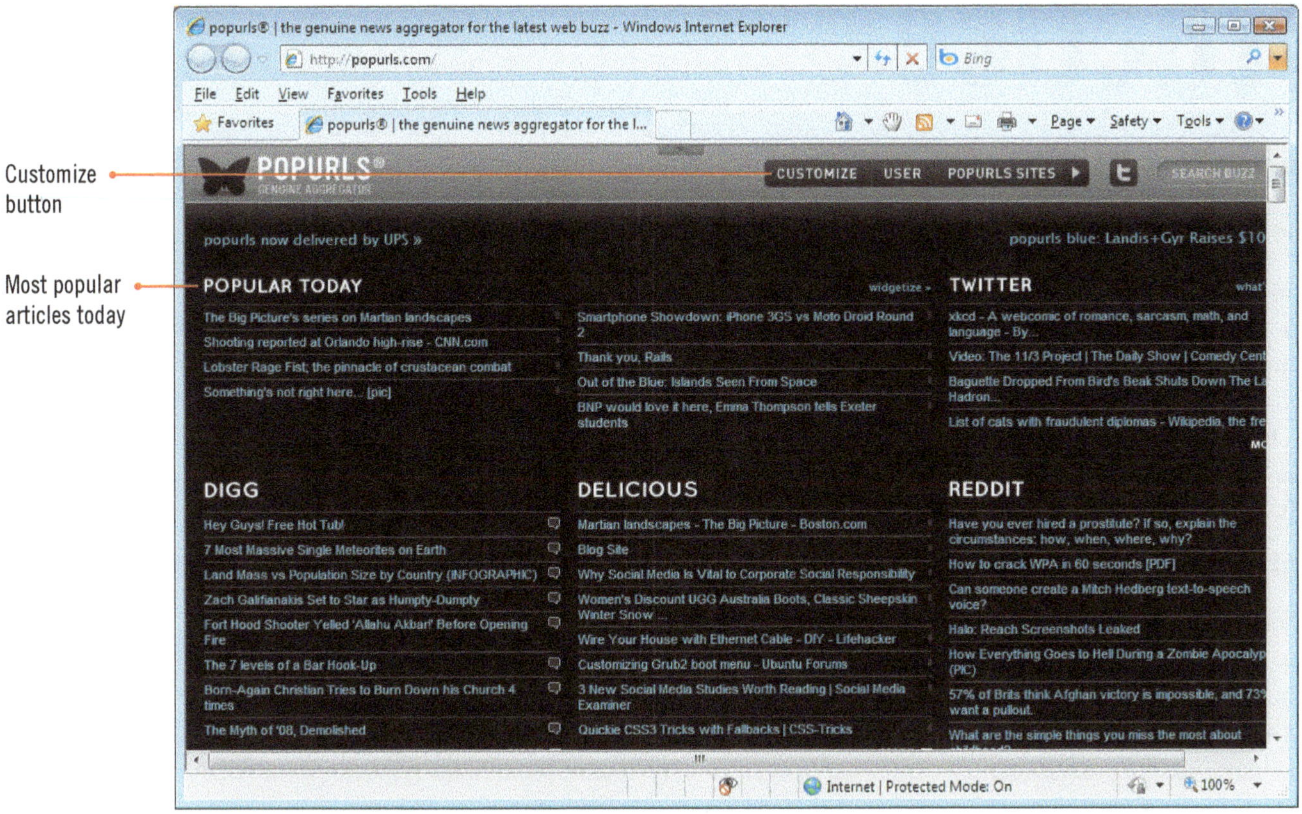

popurls.com

FIGURE D-15: Popurls blue edition for business

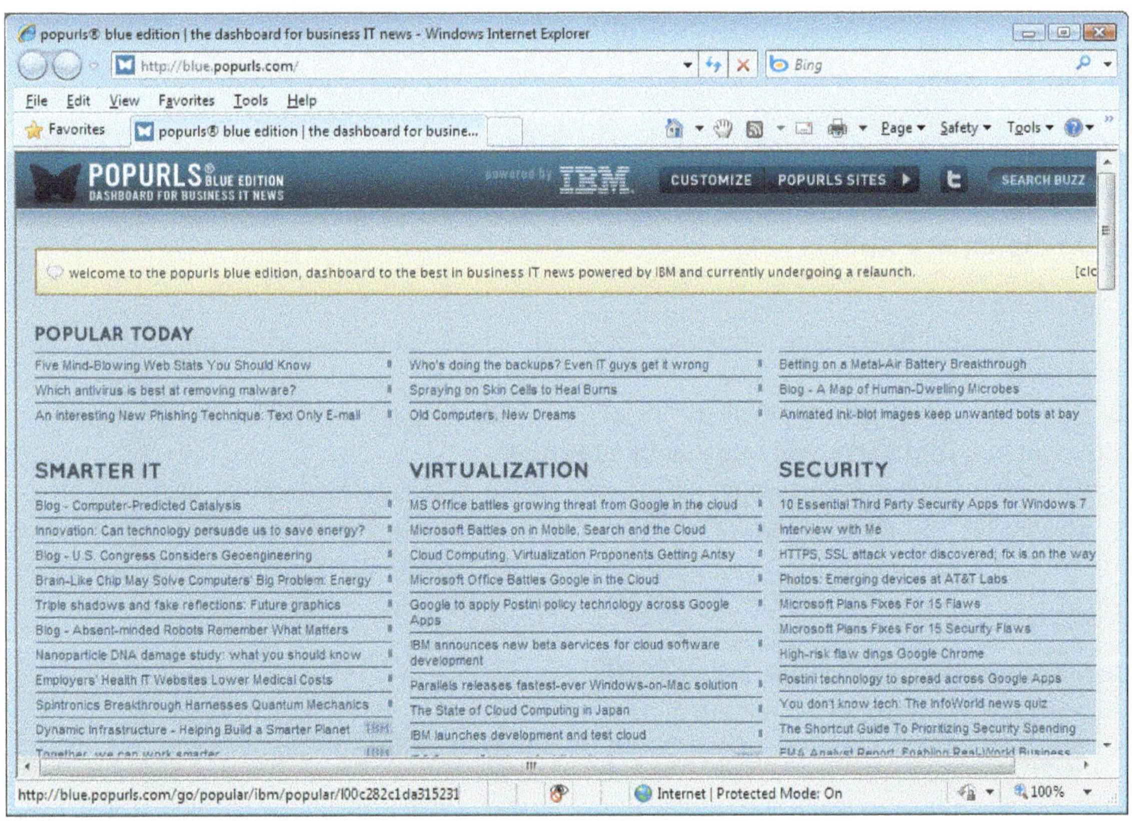

popurls.com

Professionalism

Practice

▼ SOFT SKILLS REVIEW

Understand the system.

1. **In an organization, the political culture is:**
   a. shown on the organization chart
   b. the customs, attitudes, and practices that make a company unique
   c. the group of people elected to their positions
   d. the hostility one group displays to another
2. **The person who controls access to resources in an organization is called the:**
   a. resource manager
   b. controller
   c. gatekeeper
   d. timekeeper

Identify powerful people.

1. **How do people gain power in an organization?**
   a. Through their behavior and relationships
   b. By making money
   c. Only by adding a title to their name
   d. By agreeing to all requests
2. **As a rule, people who are good at office politics:**
   a. never receive promotions
   b. are usually overlooked when others are considered for promotions
   c. receive promotions more frequently than those who are not good at office politics
   d. do not want to receive promotions

Cooperate with decision makers.

1. **Which of the following is *not* a way to cooperate with decision makers?**
   a. Exchange favors
   b. Take sole credit for a collaborative effort
   c. Offer to share
   d. Promote yourself tactfully
2. **A decision maker's territory is:**
   a. their area of control
   b. their desk and the area around it
   c. where they sell products
   d. all of the above

Develop diplomacy skills.

1. **Diplomacy is:**
   a. the art of handling situations without making others defensive or hostile
   b. the etiquette of exchanging greetings
   c. the art of dealing with people from other countries
   d. the practice of getting ahead in business
2. **How can you find a win-win solution in a conflict?**
   a. Ask participants to stop competing
   b. Separate the participants physically
   c. Ask observers to choose sides
   d. Ask the participants what they want and how they can achieve it

Choose your battles.

1. **Before engaging in a conflict, ask yourself:**
   a. whether the potential payoff is worth the cost
   b. what your manager wants you to do
   c. if you are sure you will win
   d. what your mentor would do

2. **If a colleague receives a promotion that you want, what should you do?**
   - **a.** Gossip about the colleague
   - **b.** Look for new opportunities to demonstrate your skills and abilities
   - **c.** Complain about the setback to your manager
   - **d.** All of the above

Cultivate allies.

1. **Mentors are:**
   - **a.** people who can look out for you and your career interests
   - **b.** anyone in positions of authority
   - **c.** successful professionals who are willing to meet with you to share their knowledge
   - **d.** members of the support staff
2. **Which of the following should you *not* do to cultivate allies:**
   - **a.** plan time to build relationships
   - **b.** keep a professional attitude
   - **c.** assume a casual attitude during hallway chats
   - **d.** get acquainted with all types of coworkers

Deal with negative politics.

1. **Which of the following are characteristics of negative office politics?**
   - **a.** Cordial, cooperative communication
   - **b.** Withheld information and stolen credit
   - **c.** Building power centers
   - **d.** Conflicts with others
2. **Which of the following is an effective way to resolve a negative confrontation with a coworker?**
   - **a.** Focus on company objectives
   - **b.** Vent your anger and say what you really think
   - **c.** Find fault with your coworker's opinions
   - **d.** Encourage others to take sides in the battle

Develop power and influence.

1. **Which of the following should you *not* do to develop power and influence?**
   - **a.** View power as an asset
   - **b.** Use power tactics when the stakes are low
   - **c.** Use polite persuasion
   - **d.** Do favors for others in the organization
2. **You can view power as a(n):**
   - **a.** negative feature
   - **b.** problem to solve
   - **c.** asset
   - **d.** ally

Technology @ work: Content aggregators

1. **A content aggregator is:**
   - **a.** a new type of video log
   - **b.** a Web site that collects certain types of information on the Web
   - **c.** the contents page on a popular Web site
   - **d.** a Web site that answers business questions
2. **One advantage of using a content aggregator is that it:**
   - **a.** maintains a personal profile for you
   - **b.** deletes old content from Web sites
   - **c.** sorts through your e-mail contacts
   - **d.** reduces the amount of time you take to check Web sites for updates

▼ CRITICAL THINKING QUESTIONS

1. **Have you worked in an organization where you noticed the office politics? Describe what you noticed. Did the office politics seem to be positive or negative?**
2. **Do you think you can avoid office politics on the job? If so, how? Do you think avoiding office politics offers advantages to your career?**
3. **Suppose you have been working for a company for two years. How would you go about receiving a promotion?**
4. **Consider a professional situation where you were in conflict with a coworker. How did you handle the conflict? What was the result? Would you now approach that conflict differently?**
5. **Suppose a colleague fills you in on a sensitive subject, such as a rumor that your manager will be fired. How would you respond to your colleague?**

▼ INDEPENDENT CHALLENGE 1

You are a part-time salesperson at Coffman Bakery and report directly to the owners, Dale and Greg Coffman. In addition to selling Coffman Bakery products, Dale and Greg ask you to help train new employees. Your goal is to become the sales manager at the bakery. The amount of business has grown significantly since you were hired, and you spend time each day battling problems with customers, suppliers, and employees. Dale suggests you complete the chart shown in Figure D-16 to determine which problems to battle each day.

FIGURE D-16

	High payoff	Low payoff
Few drawbacks		
Many drawbacks		

a. Use a word processer such as Microsoft Office Word to open the file **D-8.doc** provided with your Data Files, and save it as **Problem Chart.doc** in the location where you store your Data Files.
b. Read Problem Chart.doc, which describes problems you need to resolve at Coffman Bakery.
c. Complete the chart shown in Figure D-16 and provided in Problem Chart.doc by assigning each problem to a blank area of the chart.
d. Submit the document to your instructor as requested.

▼ INDEPENDENT CHALLENGE 2

As the front desk manager for Harmony Day Spa in Silver Spring, Maryland, you work directly with Louise Harper, the owner of the spa. She recently hired a new spa manager who has many years of experience running small businesses. The name of the new manager is Carrie Stohlman. Louise encourages you to develop a strong working relationship with Carrie.

a. Use a word processer such as Microsoft Office Word to open the file **D-9.doc** provided with your Data Files, and save it as **New Manager.doc** in the location where you store your Data Files.
b. Read the description of Carrie in New Manager.doc, and then list your goals for working with her.
c. Describe how you can meet your goals.
d. Submit the document to your instructor as requested.

REAL LIFE INDEPENDENT CHALLENGE

You are preparing for a job search and want to make sure your new job helps you build a successful career. Mentors and other experts can help you build your career.

a. Identify the profession or field in which you are seeking a job.

b. Use online news sources (such as *businessweek.com* or *www.nytimes.com*) or an online encyclopedia to identify experts in your field or profession. For example, suppose you are interested in starting your own business in the computer field some day. As Figure D-17 shows, you could look up information about a prominent computer business owner such as Steven Jobs in an online encyclopedia.

FIGURE D-17

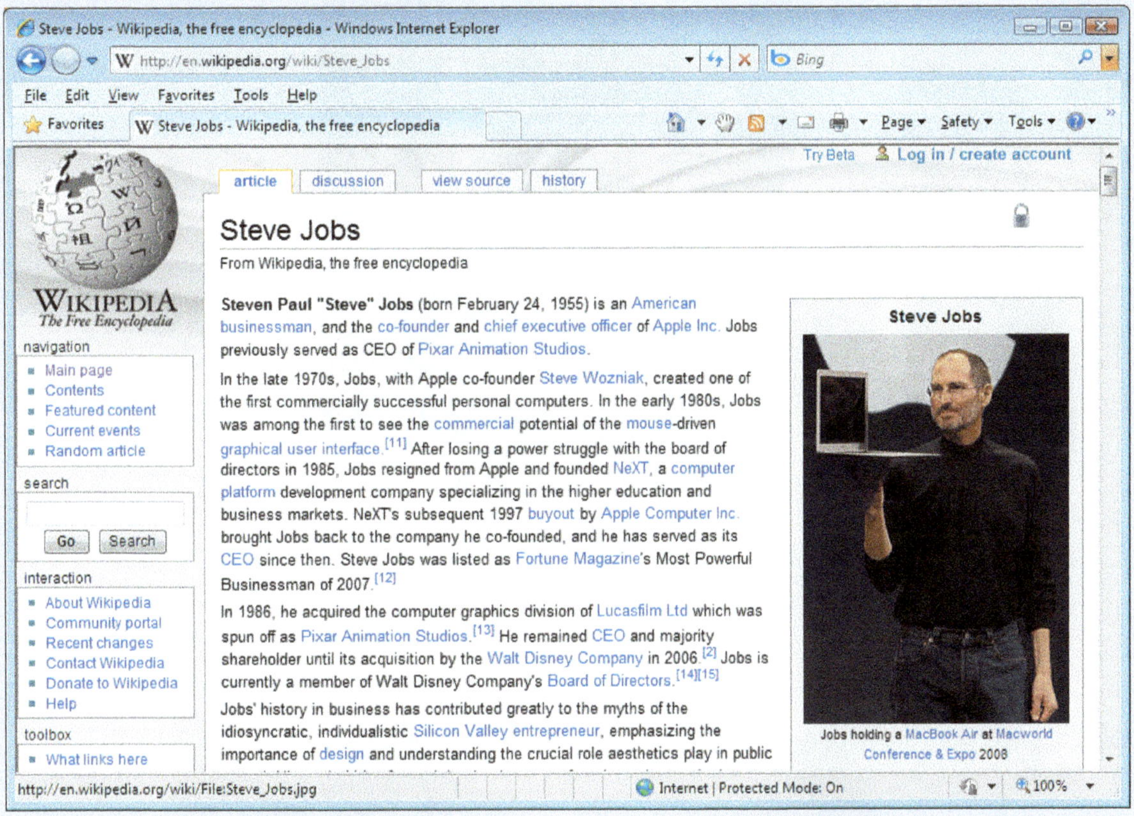

Wikipedia

c. Use this expert as a virtual mentor. Read about his or her history and find articles and books about your virtual mentor (or written by your virtual mentor).

d. Find a way to contact your virtual mentor, and send a short message describing why you selected him or her.

TEAM CHALLENGE

You are working for Clean Fields, Inc., a company in Little Rock, Arkansas that specializes in recovering polluted land. You are part of a project team studying a site near Hot Springs for a client who wants to build a shopping center. The results of the study are mixed. Some members of the team say it is safe to build on the site, while others say the land is polluted.

a. Meet and divide the members into two teams. Team A supports building on the site, while Team B opposes it.

b. Meet in your smaller teams and brainstorm reasons to build or not build on the site. Ask one person to list the reasons on a notepad or in an electronic document.

c. Meet as a larger team. Assign one person from Team A and another from Team B to debate one item on each team's list. Assign another person from Team A and Team B to debate until everyone has had a chance to debate.

d. Discuss the most effective debates. Who handled conflict diplomatically? Who avoided a negative conflict? How did they do so? Briefly summarize your discussion.

e. Send your brainstorming lists and summaries to your instructor.

▼ BE THE CRITIC

You are a new employee at UpFront Systems, a communications firm. During your first week on the job, you are crossing the courtyard to your office and see the three UpFront employees shown in Figure D-18a. The woman on the left is the manager of the other two people. Later that day, you see the UpFront employees shown in Figure D-18b. The woman in the middle is the head of the department, and the woman on the left is another new employee. Analyze the behavior and appearance of the employees in both photos. List their strengths and weaknesses in practicing positive office politics according to the guidelines in this unit. Send a list of these strengths and weaknesses to your instructor.

FIGURE D-18A

Manager of the other two employees

© Jupiterimages Corporation

a.

FIGURE D-18B

New employee

Head of a department

© Jupiterimages Corporation

b.

UNIT
E
Professionalism

Planning and Managing Your Career

Files You Will Need:

E-1.doc
E-2.doc
E-3.doc
E-4.doc
E-5.doc
E-6.doc
E-7.doc
E-8.doc
E-9.doc

If you are a full-time employee, you spend over 2000 hours every year at work. What you actually do during this time directly affects your standard of living, mental and physical health, and quality of life. More than choosing an occupation, planning your career helps you find purpose, satisfaction, and enjoyment in your work. Managing your career throughout your working life means making decisions that let you achieve your goals and reach success. Take time to find a career that interests and stimulates you, not one where you are reluctant to go to work each morning. Although you have been working at Quest Specialty Travel for a few months, you haven't taken the time to plan your career. Tia Patterson, your manager at Quest, suggests that you start managing your career. In particular, she urges you to set long- and short-term career goals so you can measure your progress and gauge your success.

OBJECTIVES

Understand career management
Research your options
Develop a long-term career plan
Set short-term career goals
Pursue training opportunities
Plan your promotions
Make career changes
Prepare to leave a job

Understanding Career Management

Many adults progress through their entire career without planning their job choices. A recent Gallup survey revealed that 7 in 10 people would seek more information on career options if they were starting over. Most reported that they found their jobs through chance, not through a series of careful decisions. People who take a job that is not a good fit for them spend half their waking hours doing work they don't enjoy. Those who plan and manage their careers tend to have higher job satisfaction and pay. Before you start working on the details of your career plans, you talk to Tia to better understand what is involved in managing a career.

DETAILS

Keep the following guidelines in mind to manage your career:

- **Think of your career as a process, not an event**
  Planning and managing your career are not one-time activities. You should continue to manage your career throughout your working life. Over time, the economy will change and occupational fields will rise and fall. People who are looking ahead, noting changes, and preparing for the next move will be more successful in the long run.

- **Take control of your future**
  Previous generations could count on employers to look out for them throughout their careers. In turn, employees loyally worked for the same company for decades. The world of work has changed. Lifelong employment is now the exception rather than the rule. According to the U.S. Bureau of Labor Statistics, professionals change jobs every 4–5 years. See Figure E-1. Take charge of your career and professional development. Otherwise, you might limit your employment options.

- **Consider personal fulfillment**
  When selecting a career, people are often motivated by prestige and compensation. As you plan your career, consider other factors important to you, such as low stress or high enjoyment. Remember that you spend more hours working than almost any other single activity. Your career should be rewarding and personally satisfying.

- **Pay attention to the details**
  Part of managing your career is fitting the details together. Table E-1 lists the qualifications for professions that require at least an associate degree. As this table shows, professions involve different types and levels of education, credentials or licenses, and skills. Some industries are concentrated in certain geographic locations. Professions also vary in salary and career tracks. Pay attention to these details so you can make the right career decisions for you.

- **Develop a wide range of skills**
  Like other Americans, you will probably work at a variety of companies and change your career during your working life. To manage these changes, develop skills that transfer from one job to another. These types of skills are called **meta-competencies**. If you focus only on education and training for your occupation, you might limit your options later. Instead, look for classes, seminars, conferences, and other opportunities to develop general skills that employers value. These include communication skills (listening, speaking, and writing), computer experience (especially using software for word processing, spreadsheets, and e-mail), and teamwork (cooperating with others).

FIGURE E-1: Years professionals remain in the same job

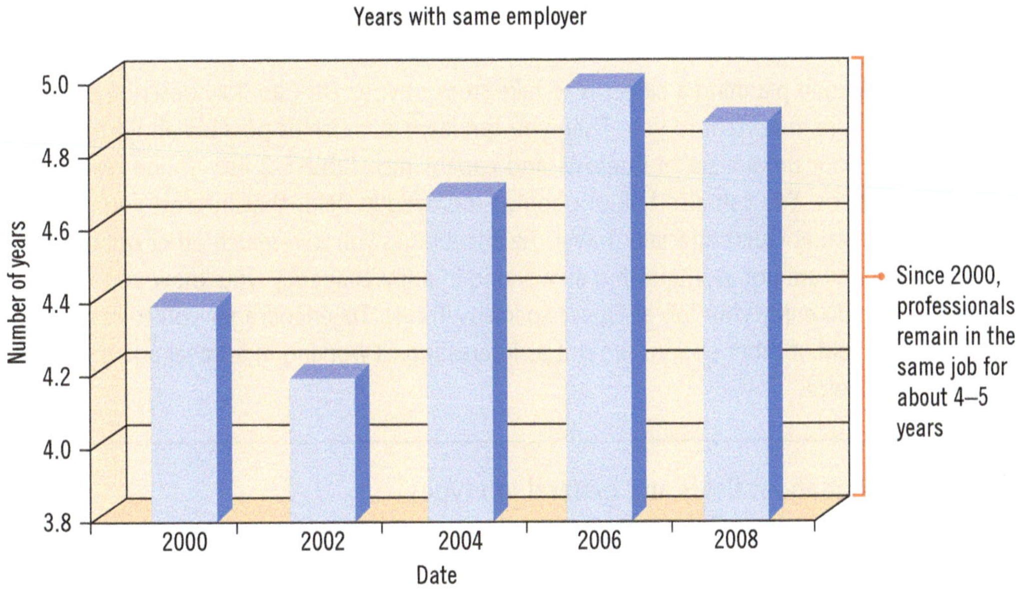

TABLE E-1: Requirements for selected professions

selected profession	minimum education	other qualifications	certification or license	required to advance
Broadcast technician	Associate degree in broadcast technology	Computer skills	Voluntary	Professional experience
Dental hygienist	Associate degree in dental hygiene	Communication skills	State license is required	Professional experience
Fashion designer	Associate degree in fashion design	Problem-solving skills	Not available	Professional experience
Library technician	Associate degree in library studies	Computer skills	Not available	Additional responsibilities
Paralegal	Associate degree in paralegal studies	Written communication skills	Voluntary	Professional experience
Social and human services assistant	Associate degree in a social or behavioral science	Communication skills	Voluntary	Formal education

Source: Occupational Outlook Handbook, 2008–2009 Edition, *www.bls.gov*.

Flexibility leads to career success

In its 2009 survey of jobs, *Money Magazine* rated the best jobs for pay and growth prospects and for quality of life, such as low stress, security, satisfaction, and benefit to society. Among the top 10 careers for pay and job growth are four jobs in the computer field (including systems engineer and network security consultant) and three jobs in the healthcare field (including nurse practitioner and physical therapist). Of those top 10 jobs for pay and growth, only two appear in the top 10 for quality of life—nurse practitioner and college professor. Are these the two best careers to pursue? Not necessarily, says Isaac Cheifetz, an executive recruiter. After analyzing the *Money* list, he says that it includes "too much health care [and] . . . too much information technology." These fields are likely to change in major ways, which will certainly affect pay, growth, and careers in general. *Money* also surveyed people in jobs that require at least a bachelor's degree. Because of international competition and the trend to move professional jobs overseas, a bachelor's degree no longer guarantees a high-quality job with good pay and growth potential. In fact, the most important credential seems to be flexibility. As the economy and jobs change, employers are looking for people that can change with the times.

Source: Staff, "Best Jobs in America," *Money Magazine*, November, 2009; Cheifetz, Isaac, "Resiliency may be the best job skill today," *Minneapolis-St. Paul Star Tribune*, November 15, 2009.

UNIT **E**

Professionalism

Researching Your Options

Your first step in planning a career is to take stock of yourself. Candidly describe the interests, skills, and values that are important to you. Then you can learn as much as possible about the careers that are well suited for your unique set of interests and capabilities. Table E-2 lists online resources for researching career options. You can also talk to people employed in fields that interest you. Although you enjoy your job at Quest Specialty Travel, Tia encourages you to research other options in the travel field. If other options are not as interesting as working in a travel agency, you know you made the right choice. Although you enjoy your job at Quest Specialty Travel, Tia encourages you to research other options in the travel field. If other options are not as interesting as working in a travel agency, you know you made the right choice.

ESSENTIAL ELEMENTS

1. **Find out about fields and general job types**

   Start learning about broad fields, and narrow down the information to jobs that you want to do. For example, suppose you are interested in travel, and have heard that hotel and lodging management is a growing field. Your goal is to know what kind of work hotel managers do, what the work environment is like, and how much you can earn. The Occupational Outlook Handbook is an excellent resource for this type of information. See Figure E-2.

2. **Learn about occupations**

   Not all occupational areas are expected to grow as much as others in the coming years. Some occupations are declining and may become extinct in the future. Consider the trends and forecasts in the occupations that interest you. Visit the U.S. Department of Labor Web site (*www.bls.gov*) to research a variety of professions and their forecasts for the coming decade.

3. **Research companies**

   If you are interested in particular companies, learn as much as you can about them. Find out basic facts, such as how long they've been in business and how many employees they have. Explore their products or services. Identify their competitors. Research their reputation and financial health. For example, if you are interested in a certain hotel chain, search for information about the company online.

4. **Request an informational interview**

   An **informational interview** is a meeting between you and a professional designed to let you learn about a company, general job requirements, or an industry. Informational interviews do not usually lead to job offers, and are more informal than job interviews. To set up an informational interview, you might call the manager of a local hotel, mention that you admire the hotel, and are considering a career in hotel management. Request a few minutes to have an informational interview with the manager on the phone or in person. Follow the same professional guidelines as you would for a job interview.

5. **Gain practical experience**

   To make sure you are really well suited for a field or occupation, gain direct experience in the field. Participate in an internship, volunteer, or work part-time to learn more about career paths and companies. If you know someone working in your field, you can shadow that person. **Shadowing** is following and observing a professional in the workplace for a day or two.

QUICK TIP
General business directories (print and online) can provide valuable information when you are researching companies.

QUICK TIP
Part-time jobs in a field are an ideal way to learn whether a job or work setting is right for you.

YOU TRY IT

1. **Use a word processor such as Microsoft Office Word to open the file E-1.doc provided with your Data Files, and save it as Options.doc in the location where you store your Data Files**
2. **Read the contents of Options.doc, which describe someone planning a career**
3. **Use the guidelines in this lesson to list ways to research career options**
4. **Save and close Options.doc, then submit it to your instructor as requested**

FIGURE E-2: General job description in the Occupational Outlook Handbook

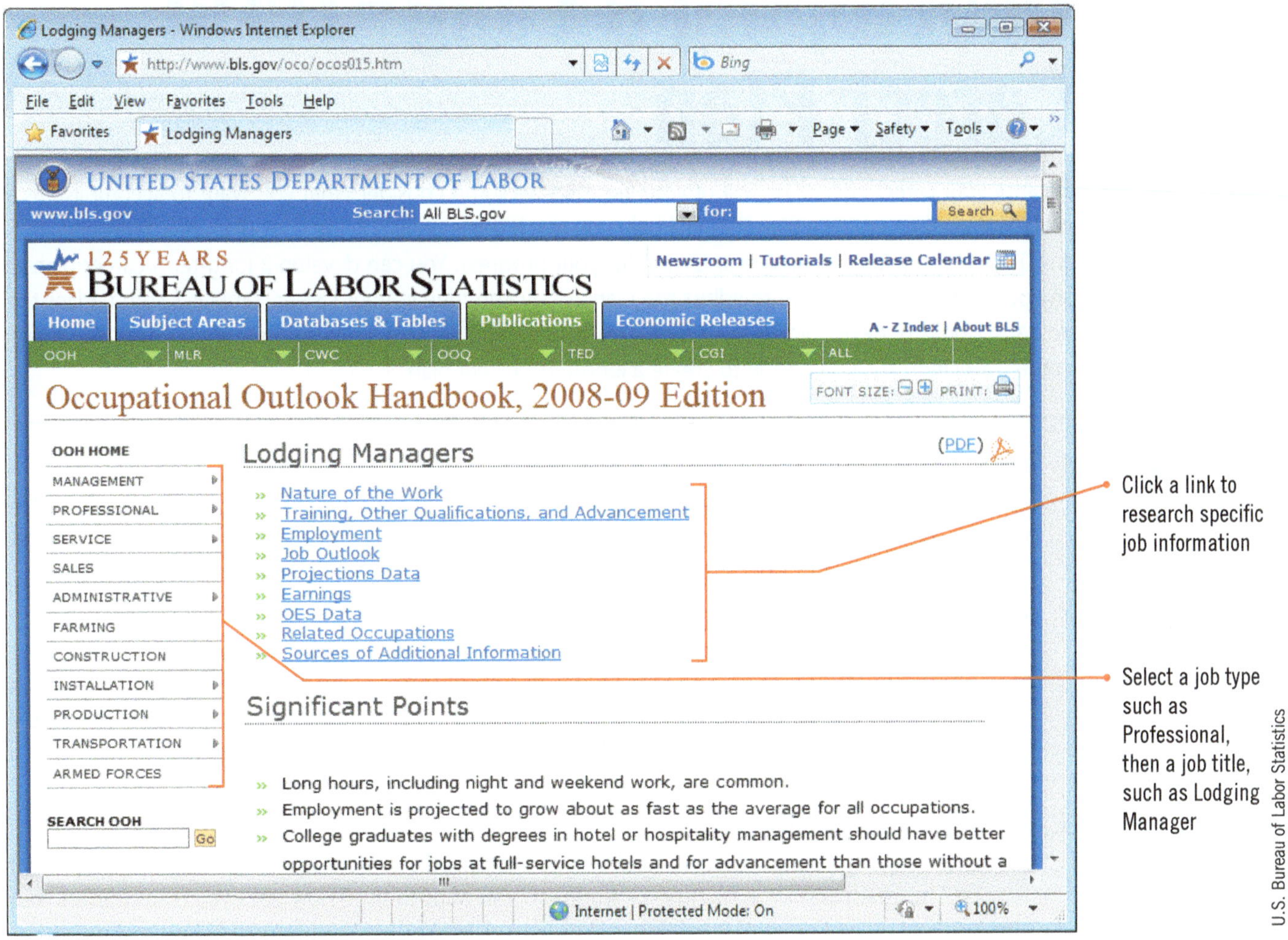

U.S. Bureau of Labor Statistics

TABLE E-2: Online resources for career research

resource	Web address	description
Career OneStop	*www.careeronestop.org*	Provides tools to help job seekers learn about careers, find jobs, and locate resources
CollegeGrad.com	*www.collegegrad.com/careers*	Lets you search for job information and provides links to other career sites
O*NET Online	*online.onetcenter.org*	Helps you identify career options based on your skills
Occupational Outlook Handbook	*www.bls.gov/oco*	Describes hundreds of different types of jobs
Riley Guide	*www.rileyguide.com*	Provides tools for researching employers and locations
WetFeet.com	*www.wetfeet.com*	Profiles career fields, employer practices, and interviewing techniques

UNIT
E
Professionalism

Developing a Long-Term Career Plan

ESSENTIAL ELEMENTS

Because your career affects the rest of your life, step back and consider what you want to accomplish as a professional. Then create a plan that will help you reach those goals. Divide your plan into milestones of 5 and 10 years so you can visualize and monitor your progress. You can develop a long-term career plan at any point in your life. Be sure to adjust the plan as you continue in your career. Table E-3 summarizes the do's and don'ts of developing a long-term career plan. After confirming that you want to remain in the travel industry, you decide to create a long-term career plan.

QUICK TIP
Without knowing what you want in life, your career progress will be largely due to chance.

1. **Set your career goals**
   Plan your career by looking ahead and deciding what you want to accomplish. List your career goals. For example, do you want to succeed in a particular type of job? Make a difference in people's lives? Become financially independent? Express yourself creatively? Include these as your career goals.
2. **List what you need to reach your goals**
   After setting your career goals, you can work backwards and determine what to do to reach those goals. For example, if your career goal is to manage a hotel, you should learn about the hotel business and work in the type of place you want to manage someday. If your goal is to be a successful tour developer, you should learn about destinations and take a job that involves a lot of travel. Figure E-3 shows the beginning of a career plan.

QUICK TIP
Your career decisions are personal choices. Stick to matters that you find important.

3. **Consider career details**
   Besides career goals, consider details that affect your working life. How much money do you need or want to make? In what part of the country (or world) do you want to live? How does your career affect your family? What is their point of view? What kind of work schedule is ideal for you? The answers to these questions help you evaluate careers and job opportunities.
4. **Include 5-, 10-, and 20-year milestones**
   Include milestones in your career plan. List your goals for 5, 10, and 20 years from now. These are also good times to evaluate your progress and adjust your plan. For example, you might want to be managing a small hotel in 5 years or leading exclusive eco-tours in 10 years. Realistically estimate how much money you want to be earning at each milestone.
5. **Adapt the plan to your actual career**
   You don't have to stick with your plan if it no longer reflects your values or makes sense for you. Feel free to take advantage of unexpected opportunities. Respond to personal, health, or family demands as necessary. In fact, you should plan for change—the company you work for may not be in business when you plan to retire. Being flexible and responsive as your situation changes will help you respond to new situations and surprises.

YOU TRY IT

1. **Use a word processor such as Microsoft Office Word to open the file E-2.doc provided with your Data Files, and save it as Plan.doc in the location where you store your Data Files**
2. **Read the contents of Plan.doc, which outline a career plan**
3. **Use the guidelines in this lesson to complete the career plan**
4. **Save and close Plan.doc, then submit it to your instructor as requested**

FIGURE E-3: Beginning of a career plan

Set your career goal

List what you need to reach your goal

Career goal:

My goal is to be the general manager of a major hotel. I want to run a profitable hotel that appeals to businesses and families, manage staff, assist in marketing and sales, and coordinate conferences.

Qualifications:

- At least an associate's degree in hotel or hospitality management
- Certification by lodging association

Required skills:

- Work as part of a team
- Get along with many types of people
- Solve problems
- Concentrate on details
- Communicate clearly
- Organize tasks
- Direct others

TABLE E-3: Developing a long-term career plan do's and don'ts

guideline	do	don't
Set career goals	• State your long-term career goals • List formal qualifications for meeting your goals • Identify skills needed to reach your goals • Consider salary, location, and schedule	• **Don't** set your sights on a career that doesn't fit your goals in other parts of your life • **Don't** disregard your family's point of view
Create a long-term plan	• Include milestones for 5, 10, and 20 years • Evaluate your progress and adjust your plan • Adapt the plan to your career as you continue to work • Respond to opportunities and demands even if they are not part of your plan	• **Don't** be unrealistic or wish for results that are unlikely • **Don't** stick with the plan if it no longer works for you—modify the plan or create a new one

Avoiding the lure of hot industries or occupations

People are often tempted to short-circuit the career-planning process and select an occupation or industry that seems prestigious or offers better-than-average compensation. Friends and family members may recommend these fields to you thinking they are offering good advice. Unfortunately, if you aren't passionate about the option, you won't be happy with it in the long run. Always base your career plan on your own value system, interests, and abilities. Passion for a job or activity usually leads to success. In fact, people often leave desirable jobs to pursue more risky ventures. The key to their success is their enthusiasm and dedication to the new job. CareerBuilder.com collects stories of people who changed careers. For example, Seth Mendelsohn writes, "I spent 7 years in the IT industry. Although it was a good job, it wasn't my real passion in life. Life is too short to have a career that I don't love, so I decided to start my own business making gourmet culinary sauces. Simply Boulder Culinary Sauces . . . has taken off and is growing at a fast rate." Another career changer, Jessi Walter, writes, "After years on Wall Street, I was laid off last summer . . . I decided to pursue my hobby of cooking with kids as a full-time venture. Today, I'm the proud owner of Cupcake Kids! . . . Needless to say, my life has done a total 180, but I couldn't be happier."

Source: Zupek, Rachel, "Success Stories: I Changed Careers," *www.careerbuilder.com,* accessed November 18, 2009.

UNIT
E
Professionalism

Setting Short-Term Career Goals

After creating a long-term career plan, set short-term goals that set you on your career path. Many of the decisions you make early in your career have a lasting effect on your success. Determine what you need to start working on today to make sure you can reach your long-term career goals later. Table E-4 lists the do's and don'ts for setting short-term career goals. As you are planning your career in the travel industry, you realize that what you most want to do is manage a hotel. You are ready to set short-term goals to achieve this ambition. See Figure E-4.

ESSENTIAL ELEMENTS

QUICK TIP
Night and online education programs make it easier to work while attending school.

1. **Get the right education**
   Most professional and skilled occupations require formal education or training. This might be a college degree, trade school program, or apprenticeship. When you researched your options, you learned the requirements of the career you want to pursue. Your first short-term goal is to get the education your career requires. For example, to run a hotel, you need a 2- or 4-year degree in hotel management.

2. **Choose the first job wisely**
   Your first professional job sets the direction of your career. It is easier to move to the next job and a higher salary if you stay in the same field. Many recent graduates accept the first position they can out of financial necessity. Try to hold out until you find a job that builds your skills in your chosen field.

3. **Determine what you need to succeed**
   Every occupation has certain qualifications for success. These might include special training, experiences, positions, or certifications. For example, in the hotel industry, assistant managers usually rotate from one assignment to another and from one hotel to another before they become general managers. Look for chances to add these qualifications to your personal portfolio.

4. **Be prepared to move**
   Many industries are concentrated in particular locations. Examples include the computer, aerospace, and automotive industries. Others, such as health care, are more universal. Learn where you can find opportunities in your field. Be prepared to move to pursue them. An ideal location has many opportunities for people in your profession.

5. **Plan to change every few years**
   In the early years of your career, you gain job-related experience, build your professional network, and add skills you need to succeed. Regularly ask yourself whether your current job is satisfying and guiding you to your long-term career goals. Changing jobs every 3–4 years offers a wide variety of experiences, can increase your compensation, and keeps the work you do fresh and interesting.

YOU TRY IT

1. **Use a word processor such as Microsoft Office Word to open the file E-3.doc provided with your Data Files, and save it as Goals.doc in the location where you store your Data Files**
2. **Read the contents of Goals.doc, which outline a career plan**
3. **Use the guidelines in this lesson to complete the short-term goals**
4. **Save and close Goals.doc, then submit it to your instructor as requested**

FIGURE E-4: Short-term career goals

Short-term career goals:

- Talk to managers at hotels Quest uses
- Talk to Tia about increasing responsibilities, especially to develop people skills
- Attend Quest training on computer software
- Learn about certification programs in hotel management
- Take hotel management courses at the local community college as a part-time student

TABLE E-4: Setting short-term career goals do's and don'ts

guideline	do	don't
Prepare for your career	• Enroll in classes or a program that your career requires • Attend training sessions related to your career • Take a job related to your career goals • Find out what your occupation expects for advancement	• **Don't** put off your education—look for part-time or flexible programs that fit your schedule • **Don't** accept the first position offered to you if it's not related to your career goals
Be flexible	• Learn where opportunities are best in your field • Be prepared to move if your industry demands it • Plan to change jobs every few years	• **Don't** move to a new location if you are unlikely to find a job there • **Don't** change jobs more frequently than every 2–3 years

Strategic job hopping

The conventional wisdom is that when the economy is slow, you should stay in your current job. But this wisdom does not apply if you are starting a career, says Penelope Trunk, author of *Brazen Careerist: Advice at the Intersection of Work and Life*. "The best thing you can do early in your career is move around a lot so you can figure out what you're good at and what you like," says Trunk. "If you compare people who job hop with people who don't, people who job hop build their network faster, build their skill set faster, and are more engaged in their work." For people who think companies will assume job hoppers are unreliable, Trunk explains, "companies actually get more passionate work out of people who are in the first 2 years at a company than people who have been there a while and plan to stay longer." In her blog (*blog.penelopetrunk.com*), Trunk qualifies this statement. "But let's be clear: Haphazard change, leaving job after job for frivolous reasons—like you want a cubicle near a window—is not going to get you far in terms of finding engaging work. But switching jobs specifically to spark more engagement in your career is smart." This is especially true for young people and certain types of jobs, such as technical jobs, which have 40% more job hopping than other fields. Job hopping with a purpose can be a way to take charge of your career.

Source: Trunk, Penelope, "Job hopping an option for young people," *Boston Globe,* March 30, 2008.

UNIT
E
Professionalism

Pursuing Training Opportunities

In many parts of the world, including the United States, what you know makes you valuable to employers. (In earlier generations, what you could do or produce was valuable.) This means employers are seeking well-educated workers. Professionals who continue to improve their knowledge through training become more valuable throughout their careers. Your career plan should include the education your occupation requires. It should also outline how to keep your working knowledge up to date. While you are working at Quest Specialty Travel, Tia encourages you to take advantage of professional training opportunities.

ESSENTIAL ELEMENTS

1. **Develop a lifelong learning attitude**

   Your career path will probably change in unexpected ways. Innovations in science and technology create new occupations. Global competition spurs rapid shifts in industries. To keep up with these changes, be prepared to refresh your knowledge. Commit to a lifelong program of learning and personal development, both formal and informal.

2. **Aim higher than the norm**

   Every occupation sets a minimum level of education. This qualification only admits you to the profession. In most cases, achieving more than the minimum requirement opens new prospects for you. For example, if most people in your field have a 2-year associate's degree, consider earning a bachelor's degree. The additional education will often tip decisions on hiring, assignments, and promotions in your favor. Figure E-5 shows how a career path follows the progress of training and education.

QUICK TIP
Some companies cover the costs of your participation in a trade or professional association.

3. **Join professional associations**

   When you begin a career, you might find that your occupation requires specialized training. For example, you might need to learn how to operate a hotel's computer network or organize conferences. Professional associations often provide this type of training. (A **professional association** is a group of people who serve a certain profession.) Associations hold workshops, seminars, trade shows, and meetings with guest speakers. Join an association for your profession so you can network and attend training sessions. Table E-5 lists a few professional associations in the United States.

QUICK TIP
Employees who participate in on-the-job training are often seen as good candidates for job promotions.

4. **Take advantage of training and education your employer offers**

   Companies usually sponsor on-the-job training to improve employee skills. Often, these short courses or workshops can lead to valuable industry certifications. Many employers also cover some or all of the cost of their employees' formal education, including degree programs. Even if your employer offers only partial support, the benefit is significant.

YOU TRY IT

1. **Use a word processor such as Microsoft Office Word to open the file E-4.doc provided with your Data Files, and save it as Training.doc in the location where you store your Data Files**
2. **Read the contents of Training.doc, which describe someone planning a career**
3. **Use the guidelines in this lesson to suggest the best type of training to pursue**
4. **Save and close Training.doc, then submit it to your instructor as requested**

FIGURE E-5: Career path and training

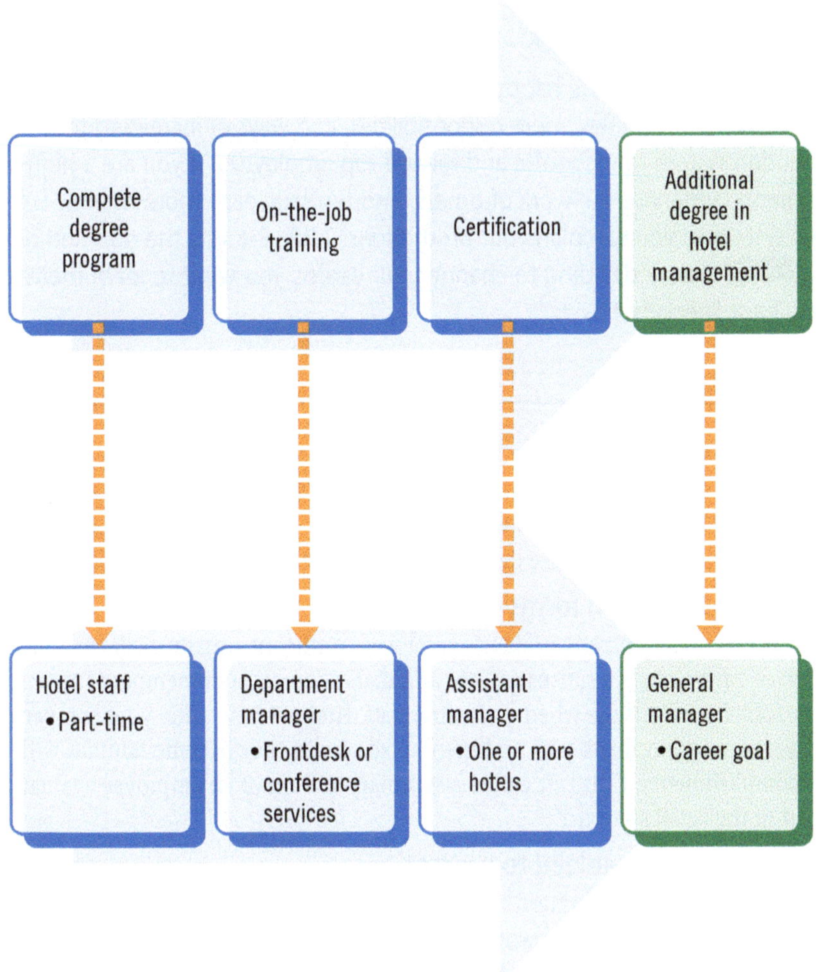

TABLE E-5: Selected professional associations in the United States

name	description	Web site
American Dental Association (ADA)	Represents the dental profession	*www.ada.org*
American Institute of Floral Design (AIFD)	Promotes floral design as a professional career	*www.aifd.org*
American Society of Travel Agents (ASTA)	Supports travel agents and the travel industry	*www.asta.org*
Hospitality Sales and Marketing Association International (HSMAI)	Serves the hospitality industry	*www.hsmai.org*
International Association for Administrative Professionals (IAAP)	Supports administrative professionals	*www.iaap-hq.org*
National Association of Fleet Administrators (NAFA)	Serves professionals who manage fleets of automobiles	*www.nafa.org*
National Association of Police Organizations (NAPO)	Serves law enforcement officers	*www.napo.org*
Painting and Decorating Contractors of America (PDCA)	Represents the painting and decorating industry	*www.pdca.org*
Professional Photographers of America (PPA)	Helps photographers advance their careers	*www.ppa.com*
Society of Broadcast Engineers (SBE)	Serves engineers in broadcast radio and television	*www.sbe.org*

UNIT
E
Professionalism

Planning Your Promotions

Few professionals would be happy doing the same job throughout their entire career. People generally seek out new opportunities, more responsibilities, and ways of increasing their salary. Most companies use a promotion system to recognize and reward top employees. If you are a high achiever, you receive new assignments, supervise the work of others, and typically earn more money. Understand your company's reward system so you can plan your promotions. Table E-6 lists the do's and don'ts for planning promotions. Before deciding to change your career, you want to learn more about the promotion system at Quest Specialty Travel.

ESSENTIAL ELEMENTS

1. **Talk to your manager**
   When you start a new position, meet with your manager and discuss what the company values and rewards. Ask your manager for advice on succeeding in your career. Make sure you understand your priorities as you begin to work. Clarify these expectations early so you are not surprised later.

2. **Examine evaluation forms**
   Learn how your company evaluates employees. Someone usually explains evaluations during your orientation to a new job. You can also talk to a human resources staff member about evaluations. Request copies of the forms managers use when evaluating staff. Find out how often your company evaluates employees. Discover who will evaluate you, and then make certain they become familiar with you, your work, and your accomplishments. Unit D includes a summary section of an employee evaluation form. Figure E-6 shows part of the detail section.

3. **Seek positions that lead to promotions**
   Advancing in an organization typically varies from one department to another. Some departments grow quickly and need additional workers, while others only replace employees who retire or leave the company. Look for departments and jobs that often lead to promotions. For example, you might accept a job as one of many assistants at a hotel because you know that company often promotes assistants.

QUICK TIP
It's often easier to ask for a lateral move than an obvious promotion.

4. **Consider all job changes**
   Not all career moves are upgrades in rank or title. Sometimes, especially early in your career, you might transfer to another department or location to perform the same job. This type of change is called a lateral move. Lateral moves can provide you with experience, training opportunities, and a new network of people. For example, if you are working in a small hotel as a front desk manager and transfer to a larger, busier hotel as a front desk manager, you are making a lateral move but improving your chances for promotion.

YOU TRY IT

1. **Use a word processor such as Microsoft Office Word to open the file E-5.doc provided with your Data Files, and save it as Promotions.doc in the location where you store your Data Files**
2. **Read the contents of Promotions.doc, which describe a company's promotion system**
3. **Use the guidelines in this lesson to suggest how to plan for promotions**
4. **Save and close Promotions.doc, then submit it to your instructor as requested**

FIGURE E-6: Detail section of employee evaluation form

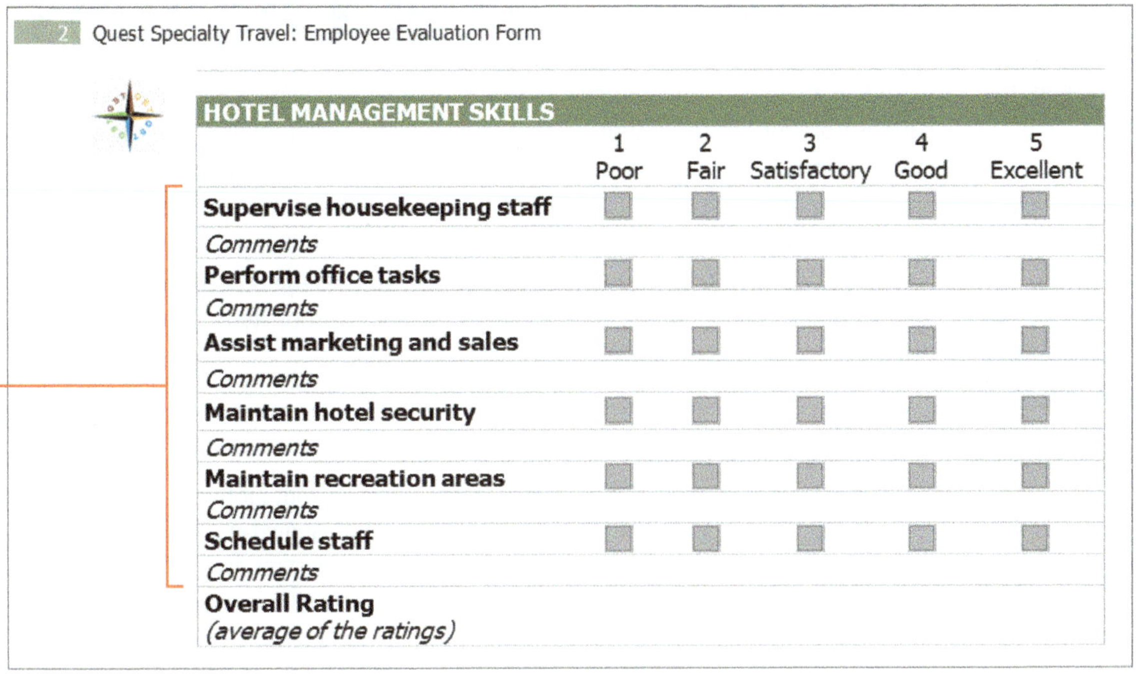
2 Quest Specialty Travel: Employee Evaluation Form

HOTEL MANAGEMENT SKILLS	1 Poor	2 Fair	3 Satisfactory	4 Good	5 Excellent
Supervise housekeeping staff	☐	☐	☐	☐	☐
Comments					
Perform office tasks	☐	☐	☐	☐	☐
Comments					
Assist marketing and sales	☐	☐	☐	☐	☐
Comments					
Maintain hotel security	☐	☐	☐	☐	☐
Comments					
Maintain recreation areas	☐	☐	☐	☐	☐
Comments					
Schedule staff	☐	☐	☐	☐	☐
Comments					
Overall Rating *(average of the ratings)*					

Concentrate on these skills to improve your chances of promotion

Quest Specialty Travel

TABLE E-6: Planning your promotions do's and don'ts

guideline	do	don't
Talk to your manager	• Discuss what the company values and rewards • Make sure you understand your priorities	• **Don't** assume you know what your manager expects of you • **Don't** be afraid of letting your manager know you want to advance in the company
Examine evaluation forms	• Learn how your company evaluates employees • Request copies of evaluation forms • Find out how often your company evaluates employees • Learn who evaluates employees	• **Don't** overlook skills on the evaluation form, especially during your first 6 months on a job • **Don't** avoid discussing your promotion chances during an evaluation
Seek positions that lead to promotions	• Observe departments and locations in your company • Note which areas promote employees frequently	**Don't** get stuck in a position with no chance of promotion—ask to be transferred or reassigned
Consider all job changes	Consider job changes that lead to more experience and training, even if they are not promotions	**Don't** dismiss lateral moves in your company

UNIT
E
Professionalism

Making Career Changes

ESSENTIAL ELEMENTS

Change is a common and natural part of professional life. Most professionals change jobs and even occupations from four to seven times during their careers. This frequency increases for younger workers. The U.S. Department of Labor statistics show that workers between the ages of 18 and 38 change jobs an average of 10 times. Changing careers can lead to greater satisfaction, flexibility, and earnings. It can also mean loss of income and instability in your life. Before changing careers, study the risks and rewards so you make a decision that is right for you. Table E-7 outlines the do's and don'ts for making career changes. After making long-term career plans and setting short-term goals, you are considering making a career change from the tour field to hotel management.

QUICK TIP

Don't make a major career decision when you are upset or emotional.

1. **Consider your reasons**
   When you are thinking about a career change, consider your motivations. Have you accomplished all that you can in your current job? Are you simply bored or frustrated at work? Are you trying to escape problems rather than solve them? Because leaving a job is an important decision, you should not make it in haste. Take stock of your skills, strengths, interests, and experiences, and analyze whether a different job or career makes sense for you.

2. **Compare the costs and benefits**
   Compare the costs or risks of making a career change against the anticipated benefits. Leaving a job can involve giving up your income and seniority. You might also lose influence and a connection to a valuable network. However, if the job change leads to the goals outlined in your career plan, the benefits might outweigh the costs. See Figure E-7.

3. **Estimate moving expenses**
   If changing a career means moving to a different place, consider the expense and complication of moving as you make your decision. When you interview for a new position, ask whether the employer covers moving expenses or offers related benefits. If you have to cover the costs yourself, add that to your cost-benefit analysis.

4. **Enroll in retraining classes**
   If your career progress is stalled, give it a kick start by retraining to review or learn the most current information in your field or in a new field. Look for part-time programs, night and weekend courses, and online classes. The U.S. Department of Labor sponsors a Web site (*www.careeronestop.org*) that helps you find retraining courses in your area. See Figure E-8.

5. **Plan ahead**
   Start planning a career move as soon as possible. Allow 6–12 months to wrap up loose ends with your current employer, secure a new position, and relocate (if necessary). You will also need additional funds to pay for these changes, so budget your resources and save what you need.

YOU TRY IT

1. **Use a word processor such as Microsoft Office Word to open the file E-6.doc provided with your Data Files, and save it as Change.doc in the location where you store your Data Files**
2. **Read the contents of Change.doc, which describe someone considering a career change**
3. **Use the guidelines in this lesson to analyze the decision**
4. **Save and close Change.doc, then submit it to your instructor as requested**

FIGURE E-7: Comparing the costs and benefits of making a career change

Stay in your current job		Change jobs without a career plan		Change jobs according to career plan	
Cost	**Benefit**	**Cost**	**Benefit**	**Cost**	**Benefit**
• Boredom • Stagnant pay • High stress	• Stability • Keep seniority • Steady income	• New job might also be boring and stressful • Lose seniority • Lose benefits	• Change can be refreshing • Short-term satisfaction • Escape problems	• Lose seniority • Lose benefits	• Work matches passion and interests • Improve chances for promotion

FIGURE E-8: Career training links

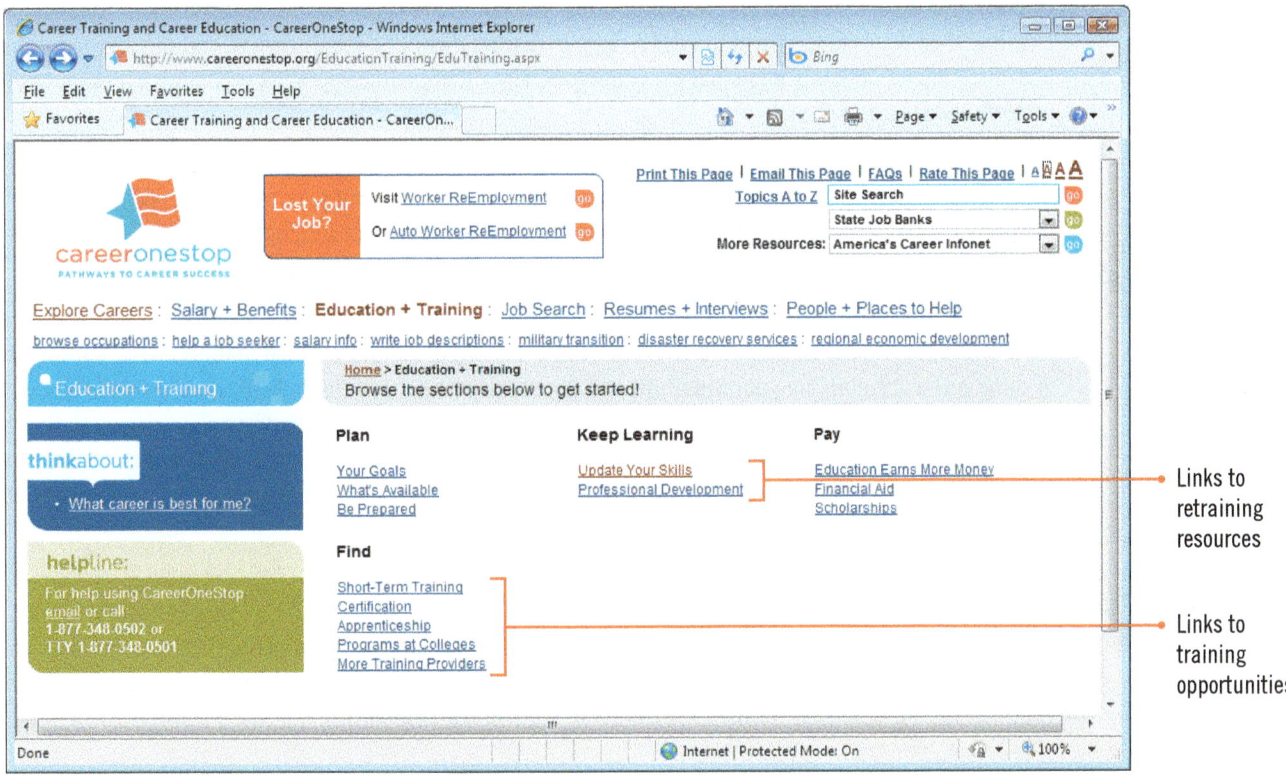

careeronestop.org

TABLE E-7: Making career changes do's and don'ts

guideline	do	don't
Consider your reasons	• List your motivations for making a career change • Analyze whether your skills, strengths, interests, and experiences are right for your current job	• **Don't** make a career change in haste • **Don't** make a decision only to escape negative parts of your job—move toward a new job that meets your career goals
Compare costs and benefits	• List the costs and benefits of your decision • Include moving costs in your analysis	• **Don't** change jobs without a clear career plan • **Don't** forget to ask your new employer about moving benefits
Plan ahead	• Prepare for a new career by retraining • Budget your income and savings to cover a career switch • Allow time to leave your current job with goodwill	• **Don't** ignore new technology and information—be one of the first at your company to gain new knowledge • **Don't** decide to make a sudden career change

Preparing to Leave a Job

ESSENTIAL ELEMENTS

In a dynamic economy, jobs are continuously being created and eliminated. Ideally, you should plan and control your career moves. However, you might need to find a new job unexpectedly. Be prepared to leave a job so that you do not suffer personal and financial losses. Table E-8 lists the do's and don'ts for preparing to a leave a job. As you continue to learn about a career in hotel management, making a career change becomes more attractive to you. You prepare to leave your job at Quest Specialty Travel.

1. **Keep your resume up to date**
   Be prepared to take advantage of an opportunity or respond to a change in job status such as a layoff. Every month or two, revisit your resume and update it with your most current title and responsibilities. Keep a current copy on a portable drive or other location where you can quickly access it.
2. **List your accomplishments**
   During your work life, you fulfill responsibilities and complete tasks. Keep a running list of these accomplishments so you can add them to your resume or discuss them in a job interview. You can also request letters of recommendation from managers, colleagues, and other people you work with and add them to your portfolio. See Figure E-9.
3. **Time your departure**
   Although some job changes are unexpected, most come with warnings. If your company experiences a downturn, you find yourself at odds with your manager, or you hear rumors of a merger or sale, begin making plans to leave. If possible, find a new job before layoffs or firings begin, which can ruin workplace morale.
4. **Resign professionally**
   No matter why you are leaving your position, resign in a dignified, professional manner. Write a short letter of resignation announcing your intention and date of departure. See Figure E-10. Don't include any other details or editorial comments. The first person to tell is your immediate supervisor. Give notice so that the company can find and train your replacement. (Notice is usually two weeks, though it varies by company.) Stay engaged and work diligently during this transition period. Be gracious in your exit, and don't say anything negative about your manager or the company to anyone.
5. **Tie up the loose ends**
   Make sure to return all company property such as cell phones, laptops, and building keys. Talk to the human resources department about any retirement accounts and receiving compensation for accrued sick and vacation time. Leave your contact information in case your previous employer needs to get in touch with you. Thank your employer for the opportunity to work at the company.

QUICK TIP
Be prepared for an employer to overreact to your resignation; some employers immediately dismiss employees who resign.

QUICK TIP
Some companies will withhold benefits if you don't comply with their resignation policies.

YOU TRY IT

1. **Use a word processor such as Microsoft Office Word to open the file E-7.doc provided with your Data Files, and save it as Leave.doc in the location where you store your Data Files**
2. **Read the contents of Leave.doc, which describe someone leaving a job**
3. **Use the guidelines in this lesson to suggest ways to improve the departure**
4. **Save and close Leave.doc, then submit it to your instructor as requested**

FIGURE E-9: Running list of career accomplishments

Start with action verbs

Include numbers

Include specific details

Career accomplishments:

- Delivered popular presentations on Quest Specialty Travel tours to school and community groups
- Developed customer service and sales skills by promoting packaged tours at travel conferences
- Trained 15 new employees in the New York office of Quest Specialty Travel
- Assisted in writing ads for local print publications
- Trained all New York employees to use updated Quest Specialty Travel computer system

FIGURE E-10: Part of a resignation letter

Announce your intention to resign

Include your date of departure

Offer to help during the transition and thank your employer

Dear Ms. Patterson:

Please accept my resignation as office assistant at Quest Specialty Travel. I have sincerely enjoyed my six months working with you and Quest, and I appreciate all that you have done for me.

I have accepted an offer with a local hotel and plan to start my new position in three weeks. I made this difficult decision because I would like to pursue opportunities in hotel management, and this position helps me meet my career goals.

I am happy to work with you to ensure a smooth transition. Again, thank you for the opportunity to be a part of Quest Specialty Travel and for the training and guidance you have provided.

TABLE E-8: Making career changes do's and don'ts

guideline	do	don't
Keep your resume up to date	• Update your resume periodically • Include a running list of accomplishments • Request letters of recommendation	• **Don't** get caught off guard • **Don't** overlook minor achievements
Time your departure	• Make plans to leave when you suspect your job status might change • Leave on good terms with your manager and colleagues • Plan to keep in touch with your coworkers	• **Don't** ignore warnings about changes in your job or company • **Don't** make statements you might later regret
Resign professionally	• Write a short letter of resignation • Tell your immediate supervisor first • Give notice, which is usually two weeks, before you leave • Stay engaged and work on your projects • Return company property • Make sure you receive all benefits due to you • Leave your contact information • Thank your employer	• **Don't** include details or editorial comments in your resignation letter • **Don't** disappear during the transition period • **Don't** say anything negative about your manager or the company

Technology @ Work: Career and Job Web Sites

ESSENTIAL ELEMENTS

The Web offers two types of resources for managing a career: career Web sites and job-hunting Web sites. Career Web sites help you research industry and occupation options, develop long-term and short-term plans, and learn about details such as salary expectations. Many career Web sites are sponsored by the federal government, such as Career OneStop (*www.careeronestop.org*) and the Bureau of Labor Statistics (*www.bls.gov*). Besides helping you find a job, job-hunting Web sites also provide career tools and articles about managing your career. For example, Yahoo Careers (*https://careers.yahoo.com*) provides career articles about resumes, interviewing, salary, and networking. Before you leave Quest Specialty Travel, you offer to show Tia what you've learned about career and job-hunting Web sites.

1. **Assess yourself**
   Use career and job Web sites to take stock of your interests, skills, strengths, and goals. For example, a page on the Career OneStop Web site (*www.careerinfonet.org*) guides you to create a profile of yourself. You list your skills and then match them to job types that need those skills. See Figure E-11.

2. **Create career plans**
   Many sites include tools that help you develop career plans. For example, CareerBuilder.com provides a tool called CareerPath (*www.careerpath.com*). You take one or more quizzes and then review the results as you decide on a career path, learn about career choices, and rate your job satisfaction. See Figure E-12.

3. **Find training resources**
   Although the best training resources are usually local education centers such as community colleges, you can narrow your search using a career Web site. For example, Career OneStop helps you find education and training programs where you can earn a certificate, diploma, or award in less than two years. You search by occupation, school, or type of program.

4. **Find job information**
   Because so many people post resumes on the major job-hunting Web sites such as Monster.com (*www.monster.com*) and JobCentral.com (*www.jobcentral.com*), your chances are very slim that you'll find a job through one of these sites. However, you can find information that is useful for job searches, such as the types of job openings employers are posting, the qualifications employers are looking for, and salary information for specified occupations.

QUICK TIP
To find job Web sites, use a search term such as "Top 10 job sites," and then compare one site to another.

YOU TRY IT

1. **Open a Web browser such as Microsoft Internet Explorer or Mozilla Firefox, and go to** www.careerinfonet.org
2. **Click** Explore Careers, **then click** Find Assessments **in the Self Assessments list**
3. **Click** Skills Profiler, **then complete the quiz to profile your skills**
4. **Take a screenshot of the results and send it to your instructor as requested**

FIGURE E-11: Assessing your skills at the Career OneStop Web site

Click to explore careers

Follow the steps to complete a skills profile

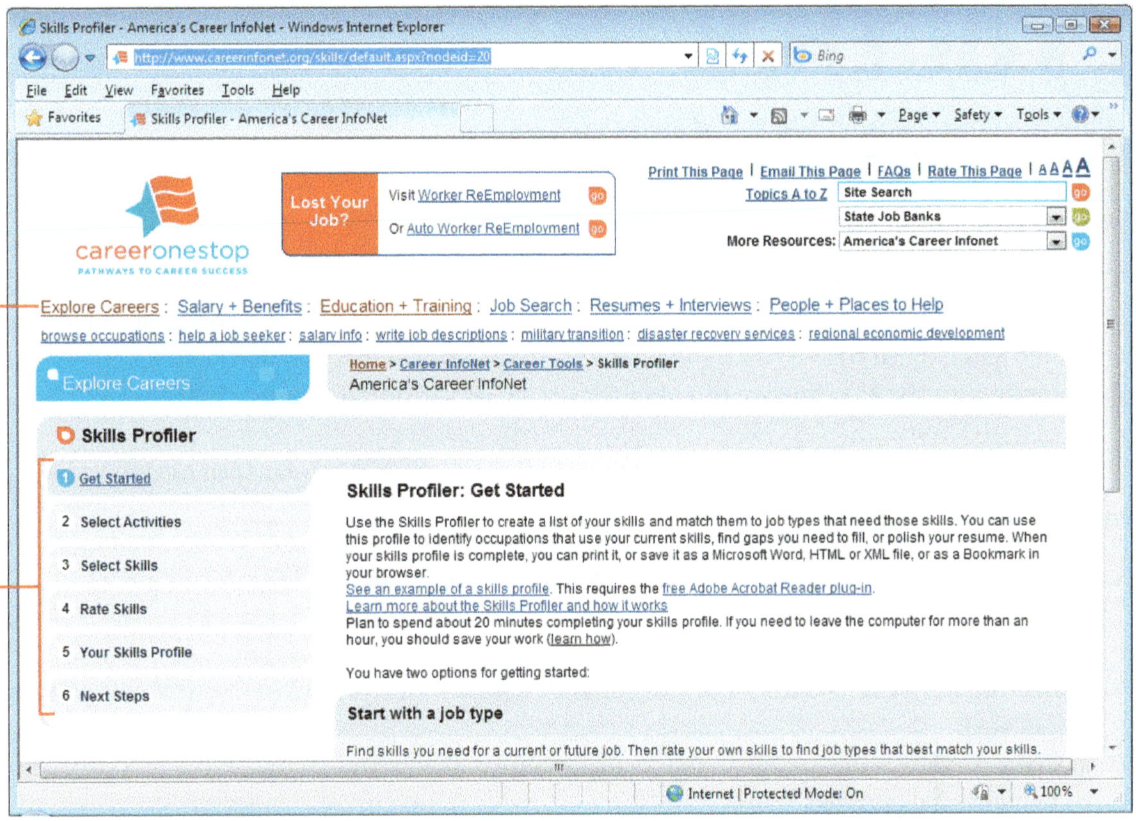

careeronestop.org

FIGURE E-12: Career quizzes at CareerPath

Select a quiz to help you develop a career plan

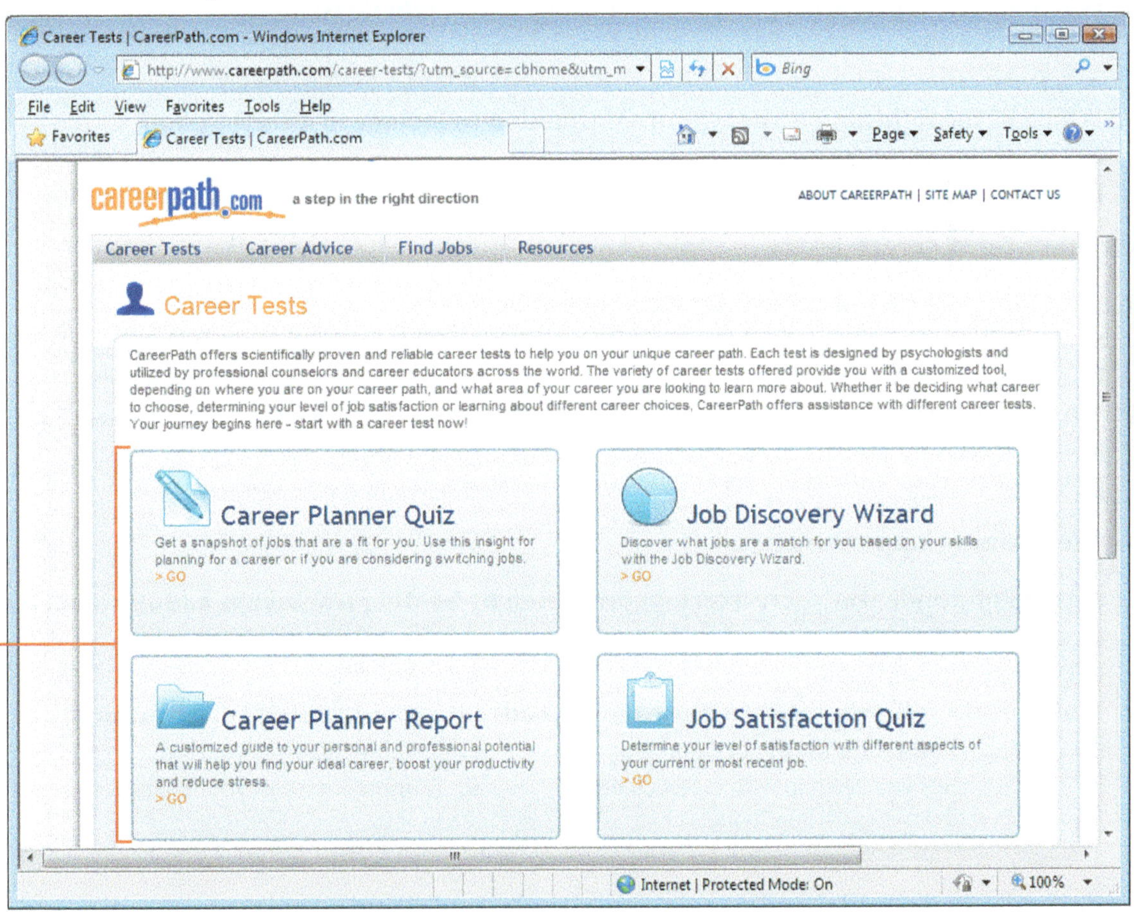

careeronestop.org

Practice

▼ SOFT SKILLS REVIEW

Understand career management.

1. **People who plan and manage their careers:**
   a. regret their choices
   b. find jobs through chance
   c. have higher job satisfaction and pay
   d. take jobs they don't enjoy
2. **According to the U.S. Bureau of Labor Statistics, professionals change jobs:**
   a. every 4–5 years
   b. every 4–5 months
   c. rarely
   d. once or twice in their careers

Research your options.

1. **Which of the following should you *not* research when you are planning a career?**
   a. Job types
   b. Occupations
   c. Companies
   d. Resignation letters
2. **A meeting between you and a professional designed to let you learn about a company or field is called a(n):**
   a. career profile
   b. informational interview
   c. shadow
   d. occupational interview

Develop a long-term career plan.

1. **When developing a career plan, the first thing you should do is:**
   a. write a resume
   b. set your career goals
   c. plan your promotions
   d. apply for internships
2. **Which of the following is the type of information to include in a career plan?**
   a. List of hot occupations
   b. Strategies to win the state lottery
   c. Occupations that don't match career goals
   d. Skills to develop to reach your goals

Set short-term career goals.

1. **Most professional and skilled occupations require:**
   a. education or training
   b. moving to a different city
   c. informational interviews
   d. unusual meta-competencies
2. **Which of the following is *not* a qualification occupations might require for success?**
   a. Certification
   b. Special training
   c. Internship
   d. Certain types of experience

Pursue training opportunities.

1. **A group of people who serve a certain profession by holding workshops and seminars is called a(n):**
   a. industry or field
   b. professional association
   c. career planner
   d. apprentice
2. **Which of the following is *not* a reason to take advantage of training opportunities?**
   a. Training relieves the boredom of a dull job
   b. Training helps you keep up with career changes
   c. Training increases your value to your employer
   d. Training increases your chances to be hired or promoted

Plan your promotions.

1. **What do most companies use to recognize and reward top employees?**
   - **a.** Training opportunities
   - **b.** Certification programs
   - **c.** Promotion system
   - **d.** Apprenticeships
2. **What type of career change can provide experience, training opportunities, and a new network of people without involving a promotion?**
   - **a.** Lateral move
   - **b.** Backwards move
   - **c.** Balance move
   - **d.** Evaluation

Make career changes.

1. **Before making a career change, you should:**
   - **a.** calculate how long you've had the same job
   - **b.** focus on the rewards, not the risks
   - **c.** compare the costs to the benefits
   - **d.** earn a promotion
2. **Changing careers can lead to:**
   - **a.** greater job satisfaction
   - **b.** loss of income
   - **c.** higher salary
   - **d.** all of the above

Prepare to leave a job.

1. **Because your job status can change unexpectedly, what should you do to prepare to leave a job?**
   - **a.** Update your resume
   - **b.** List your accomplishments
   - **c.** Request letters of recommendation
   - **d.** All of the above
2. **What should you *not* do when writing a letter of resignation?**
   - **a.** Announce that you are resigning
   - **b.** Mention the date you are leaving
   - **c.** Critique your manager
   - **d.** Thank your employer

Technology @ Work: Career and job Web sites

1. **Which of the following can you *not* do on a career or job Web site?**
   - **a.** Conduct an informational interview
   - **b.** Assess your skills and interests
   - **c.** Create career plans
   - **d.** Research salaries
2. **Why should you use the major job-hunting Web sites?**
   - **a.** Your chances are high that you'll find a job on the site
   - **b.** You can learn about the types of job openings employers are posting
   - **c.** Employers tend to use the sites more than other methods to find employees
   - **d.** They provide certification in career planning

▼ CRITICAL THINKING QUESTIONS

1. **Some people find that planning a career removes the spontaneity and fun from an important part of life. They also think career plans make people rigid. Do you agree? Why or why not?**
2. **Think about jobs you've had in your life. Which do you consider your best jobs? What made them a good fit for you? Which qualities do you plan to seek in other jobs?**
3. **Explain how a career, a job, and an occupation are different from one another.**
4. **Suppose you work for a company named SmallBiz. A colleague tells you he read a rumor on the SmallBiz blog that a larger company is buying SmallBiz. What do you do?**
5. **Opinions vary about when you should tell an employer you are planning to leave. If you give two-weeks notice before you have a new job, your employer might fire you immediately. On the other hand, if you search for a job while employed, you might need to use time during the workday to meet with potential employers. What are the pros and cons of both approaches? How do you plan to handle this situation in your career?**

▼ INDEPENDENT CHALLENGE 1

Dale and Greg Coffman are brothers who own Coffman Bakery in Barrington, Illinois. You have been working at the bakery as a part-time salesperson for a few months, and want to continue your career in sales. Dale encourages you to pursue a career as a sales representative for wholesale bakery items. He suggests you research this career path in the Occupational Outlook Handbook. See Figure E-13.

FIGURE E-13

U.S. Bureau of Labor Statistics

a. Use word-processing software such as Microsoft Office Word to open the file **E-8.doc** provided with your Data Files, and save it as **Sales Rep.doc** in the location where you store your Data Files.
b. Using a Web browser, go to the home page for the Occupational Outlook Handbook at *www.bls.gov/oco*.
c. Find information under **Sales Representatives, Wholesale and Manufacturing**, as shown in Figure E-13.
d. Based on the information you find, complete the career description in Sales Rep.doc.
e. Submit the document to your instructor as requested.

▼ INDEPENDENT CHALLENGE 2

You are the part-time front desk manager for the Harmony Day Spa in Silver Spring, Maryland. Louise Harper is the owner of the spa. She knows you are working at the spa only as you finish your education, and asks about your career plans. Your goal is to work as a physical therapist assistant. Louise offers to help you create a long-term career plan. So far, you have listed your career goals. See Figure E-14.

FIGURE E-14

> **Career goal:**
>
> My goal is to work as a physical therapist assistant to provide treatments and exercises that help patients improve their mobility, relieve pain, and prevent injuries.
>
> **Qualifications:**
>
> •
>
> **Required skills:**
>
> •

a. Use word-processing software such as Microsoft Office Word to open the file **E-9.doc** provided with your Data Files, and save it as **Career Plan.doc** in the location where you store your Data Files.
b. Using the online resources mentioned in this unit, research the career of a physical therapist assistant.
c. In Career Plan.doc, list the qualifications and required skills needed to reach this goal.
d. Submit the document to your instructor as requested.

▼ REAL LIFE INDEPENDENT CHALLENGE

You can use the online resources discussed in this unit to learn about occupations that interest you.

a. On your own or using a Web site such as Career OneStop (*www.careeronestop.org*) or CareerBuilder.com (*www.careerbuilder.com*), identify up to five interests and skills that you have.
b. List two or three occupations that match your interests and skills.
c. Select the first occupation and learn the following information about it:

- Type of work people do in the occupation
- Training requirements
- Job outlook
- Typical earnings

d. Do you want to include this occupation as a career goal? If not, select the second occupation and learn the same information about it as listed in the previous step.

▼ TEAM CHALLENGE

You are working for Clean Fields, Inc., a company in Little Rock, Arkansas specializing in recovering land that has been contaminated or polluted. You have the education and skills that this job requires, but you are ready to make a career change. You are very interested in green careers. Your project team offers to help you identify your options.

a. Research the types of jobs people have in green careers. List five jobs and bring the list to a team meeting.
b. During the meeting, assign one job to each team member.
c. Independently, learn about the education and skills required for your job. Also learn about the nature of the work, job prospects, and career path.
d. Work again as a team and discuss your findings. Also discuss the pros and cons of each job you researched.

▼ BE THE CRITIC

You just completed your education at a community college and are considering your career options. You start by creating the career plan shown in Figure E-15. Using the online resources discussed in this unit, research a career as a paralegal. Learn about the nature of the work and the education, interests, and skills required for the job. Then evaluate the strengths and weaknesses of the career plan. Send a list of the strengths and weaknesses to your instructor as requested.

FIGURE E-15

Career plan:

I like working with people and being creative. My family is encouraging me to work in the legal field, so I have chosen the career of a legal assistant.

- My uncle is a lawyer
- I have an associate's degree in graphic design
- Work as part of a team
- Develop my writing skills (weak)
- Solve problems
- Concentrate on details
- Use computer software (strength)
- Organize tasks
- Summer employment with my uncle
- High school computer training
- Experience working with a team (school project)
- Find out about certification
- Goal is to work in a small law office
- Prefer job with flexible or shorter hours

Glossary

Assimilate To blend sounds together in speech.

Blog A special type of Web page where you can post commentary, event descriptions, or material.

Business casual A style of dress that usually means attire less formal than a traditional suit and tie, yet dressier than jeans and a t-shirt.

Chain of command The line of authority in a military unit through which orders are passed. In business, the chain of command defines who supervises and is responsible for the work of others.

Clique A tight knit group of people with common values and identities.

Content aggregator A Web site that collects certain types of information on the Web.

Dependable A quality related to reliability, honesty, and trustworthiness that shows someone can be counted on to deliver something or complete a task as promised.

Diction The degree of clarity and proper pronunciation in your speech.

Diplomacy The art of handling situations without making others defensive or hostile.

Domain name The label used to identify a site on the Internet, such as *softskills.org* or *whitehouse.gov*.

Elevator speech A basic introduction about yourself that takes as long as an elevator ride (from 30 seconds to 2 minutes) and includes your name, information about your company, position, and what you do, and details important or interesting to the person you are meeting.

Entrepreneur Someone who starts a new business, often risking their own investments of time and money.

Ergonomics The science of designing your workspace to fit you and your body.

Gatekeeper The person in an organization who controls access to resources ranging from basic office supplies to complex computer programs.

Image How you combine clothing, grooming, behavior, and speech to represent yourself to others.

Informational interview A meeting between you and a professional designed to let you learn about a company, general job requirements, or an industry.

International business attire A style of dress that includes suits, jackets, dresses, long-sleeved shirts, ties, and leather shoes.

Mentor A teacher or trusted counselor.

Meta-competencies Skills that transfer from one job to another.

Online persona The publicly searchable information available about you on the Internet.

Organization chart A diagram showing the structure of an organization.

Personal hygiene The practice of maintaining cleanliness and health.

Political culture The customs, attitudes, and practices that make a company unique.

Professional association A group of people who serve a certain profession.

Professional networking Practices for creating and cultivating business friendships.

Protocol A rule for carrying out an action or behavior.

Reliable Ability to perform a job under routine circumstances and act responsibly when the unexpected occurs.

Shadowing Following and observing a professional in the workplace for a day or two.

Sleep debt A condition of physical and mental fatigue that occurs when you work too much and fail to get enough rest.

Social bookmarking A way to organize and share links to Web sites and other online resources.

Social protocol A generally understood and accepted way that governs how people interact with each other.

Stakeholder A person who is affected by a problem or decision or whose involvement you need to resolve the matter.

Stress A body's response to difficult or dangerous situations.

Territory The area of control, such as employees, physical space, spending, or a step in the approval process.

Time management A set of tools and techniques you can use to schedule your time and accomplish particular tasks, goals, and projects.

Verbal fluency Ease in speaking, especially during conversations.

Work ethic Personal characteristics such as dependability, initiative, effort, responsibility, integrity, and punctuality.

Index

A

B

C

D